OUTDOOR ESCAPES
New York City

Help Us Keep This Guide Up to Date

Every effort has been made by the author and editors to make this guide as accurate and useful as possible. However, many things can change after a guide is published—trails are rerouted, regulations change, techniques evolve, facilities come under new management, and so on.

We would love to hear from you concerning your experiences with this guide and how you feel it could be improved and kept up to date. While we may not be able to respond to all comments and suggestions, we'll take them to heart and we'll also make certain to share them with the author. Please send your comments and suggestions to the following address:

The Globe Pequot Press
Reader Response/Editorial Department
P.O. Box 480
Guilford, CT 06437

Or you may e-mail us at:

editorial@globe-pequot.com

Thanks for your input, and happy travels!

A **FALCON** GUIDE®

OUTDOOR ESCAPES SERIES

OUTDOOR ESCAPES
New York City

Theodore W. Scull

FALCON®

GUILFORD, CONNECTICUT
HELENA, MONTANA

AN IMPRINT OF THE GLOBE PEQUOT PRESS

Text design: Lisa Reneson
Maps: Tim Kissel/Trailhead Graphics, Inc.; © The Globe Pequot Press
Photo credits: All interior photos courtesy of the author.

Library of Congress Cataloging-in-Publication Data
Scull, Theodore, W., 1941–
 Outdoor escapes New York City / by Theodore W. Scull—1st ed.
  p. cm. — (A Falcon guide) (Outdoor escapes series)
 ISBN 0-7627-0935-9
 1. Outdoor recreation—New York (State)—New York—Guidebooks. 2. Hiking—New York (State)—New York—Guidebooks. 3. Cycling—New York (State)—New York—Guidebooks. 4. New York·(N.Y.)—Guidebooks. I. Title. II. Series. III. Series: Outdoor escapes series

GV191.42.N7S38 2003
917.47'104—dc21   2002041645

Manufactured in the United States of America
First Edition/First Printing

To New York City, home sweet home.

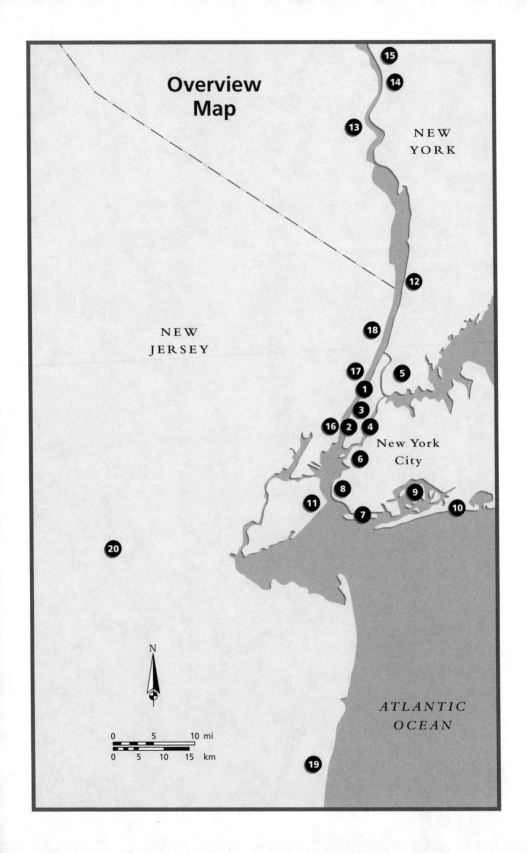

Overview
Map

15

14

13

NEW
YORK

12

NEW
JERSEY

18

17 5

1

3

16 2 4

New York
City

6

8 9

11 7 10

20

N

ATLANTIC
OCEAN

0   5   10 mi
0   5   10   15 km

19

Contents

Introduction

Residing in a densely populated city of eight million, thoughts of the great out-of-doors often seem about as remote as a trip to the moon. But there is hope for us all.

New York has always been a visionary city, hence a place of great achievements—the Brooklyn Bridge, Empire State Building, Broadway, Wall Street, Central Park—my front yard, my backyard.

Between the mid–nineteenth and early twentieth centuries, folks with foresight knew that the fast-growing metropolis would eventually gobble up all remaining open spaces, so they fought and bought and contributed to the preservation and creation of some fantastic wonders of nature that we still enjoy today, either within the five boroughs or just an hour or two away from the city by train, ferry, bus, or car.

Central Park qualified as the crown jewel of nineteenth-century New York, and this truly wonderful place remains so today. Manhattan's marvel begat its counterpart, the more rural Prospect Park in Brooklyn, followed by slim, sinuous Riverside Park on Manhattan's West Side and the great expanse of Van Cortlandt Park, once part of a family estate in the Bronx. It may be hard to believe, but a true wildlife refuge exists in Queens—the borough that defines *urban sprawl*—located smack in the middle of Jamaica Bay. Birds traveling the Atlantic Flyway began stopping over from the day it opened. Some even became permanent residents.

Just across the George Washington Bridge, the creation of Palisades Interstate Park saved the magnificent Hudson Valley cliffs from destruction through the mining of stone and the felling of trees. Bear Mountain–Harriman State

Outdoor escapes can be as close as rural Prospect Park in Brooklyn, as seen here through the Endale Arch.

Park's 52,000 wooded acres are crisscrossed by 235 miles of marked trails; from east to west, it takes two days of hard hiking to traverse all this wilderness, all within an hour's drive from New York City.

There are human-made structures to enjoy, too. The first Croton Aqueduct, completed in 1842 to solve the city's freshwater supply problems, today provides a 30-mile, continuous linear trailway from the Bronx to Croton Dam in northern Westchester County. The Delaware & Raritan Canal, dating from 1834, provides 60 miles of towpath trails and a waterway for canoeing, kayaking, and fishing. The boardwalks of Brooklyn, the Rockaways, Staten Island, and the North Jersey Coast make terrific sea-air outings for cyclists and hikers. As I write, I am thinking of a distant sunny Presidents' Day weekend when my wife and I took the train to Spring Lake, New Jersey. On the second morning, we walked to the boardwalk, looked north, and oh so far away the Asbury Park skyline appeared like a beckoning speck on the horizon. Traveling with backpacks, we set out, and 7 brisk sand-and-sea miles later we had discovered a great hike and the Victorian treasure of Ocean Grove, then returned home from the Asbury Park station. Since then we have become reg-

This rocky cut along the Old Croton Aqueduct Trailway makes for a scenic hike above the Croton River in Westchester County.

ular visitors to Spring Lake and Ocean Grove.

Outdoor escapes need not be limited to seeking nature in the mountains and woods and at the seashore. I have found exhilarating escapes hiking and cycling the bridges of New York. Nearly everyone knows about the view from the Brooklyn Bridge, but what about the Manhattan, Williamsburg, Queensboro, George Washington, Henry Hudson, and Pulaski Bridges? They all provide platforms from which to observe the city, and traffic congestion does not determine how long you have to enjoy the sights. Bridges lead you to neighborhoods—Chinatown, Polish Greenpoint, upscale Brooklyn Heights— and one offbeat itinerary here takes in five over-the-river spans.

The ultimate urban hike is to march the entire length of Broadway from the Battery into the Bronx—18 miles of ever-changing New York: the Canyon of Heroes, the recycled industrial architecture in Soho, the Village, Macy's, Times Square, the theater district, the Upper West Side, Spanish Harlem, the Bronx under the el, and Van Cortlandt Park. I led a group of fifty hikers one November day, and forty-eight made it all the way to Yonkers and received certificates to prove it.

Most New Yorkers know the subway or bus that takes them to work and maybe how to get to the Village or Chinatown, but may be utterly mystified about how to reach the Hudson Highlands, a real beach that is not Coney Island, or the other side of the Hudson without a car. It's also a fact that only 23 percent of New Yorkers own a car. I have lived here all my working life and never even considered buying one. I have a convenient rental office 4 blocks away that I frequent maybe twice a year!

Renting a car on weekends in Manhattan or Brooklyn is more expensive than during the week because of demand (just the opposite of the rest of the country), and a summer rental costs upward of $100 a day, factoring in the gas and tolls. It's still cheaper, and often more pleasurable, to take the train to the Jersey Shore than to fight your way out of the city and then endure the dull Jersey Turnpike and Garden State Parkway. Enjoy a one-way hike from Ocean Grove to Spring Lake, and ride the train back in ten to fifteen minutes.

Unlike Los Angeles, Miami, or Atlanta, New York's public transportation system was built to carry people of all incomes into and around the city, and to take its residents out to the countryside and beaches. It still does so. Many beach resort towns such as Spring Lake and Ocean Grove initially drew outward travel from the city, but lately they have become bedroom suburbs, too, so daily travel goes both ways.

Every outing chosen for this book can be accessed conveniently by public transportation. I'll take you by the hand from the minute you climb aboard a Hudson Line train at Grand Central to spend the day hiking the Old Croton Aqueduct Trailway, or perhaps suggest you ride an (elevated) subway where you begin to smell the salt air before you even see the beach.

Drivers get the best directions, too: where to park, how not to have to hike back the same way, and when not to take the car at all—such as walking from park to park in Brooklyn or cycling from the Battery along the Hudson to the 79th Street Boat Basin.

The chapters are laid out to first let you know what kind of outing it is—most involve hiking and cycling, but you'll also find in-line skating, kayaking, canoeing, and swimming—how long it is, how difficult, the best time to go, and what to take along. A section helps you get there and back, always by train, bus, or ferry, and by car when it's a sensible alternative.

The Introduction provides the attractions of each outing, historical background, and anecdotes. It may be a mystery why anyone would want to walk clear across the Bronx, but read about the kaleidoscope of neighborhoods and

Canoeing provides an alternative outdoor experience along the Delaware and Raritan Canal at Griggstown, New Jersey.

decide for yourself. Perhaps you have taken the train up the Hudson but never thought of getting off to hike up Bear Mountain, a place that you have only seen through the window. Or maybe you have driven across the George Washington Bridge but never knew you could walk or cycle across it, turn right to spend a day hiking and cycling the Palisades, or turn left to explore a string of communities poised under and perched atop the cliffs.

The Itinerary lays out the day, giving a full description from the starting point to the bitter end. Step-by-step instructions and directions will navigate you from Coney Island to Brighton Beach to Manhattan Beach and Sheepshead Bay; when the Croton Aqueduct Trailway is suddenly blocked by Sleepy Hollow High School, I'll tell you how to get around the obstruction and continue on your way. Virtually none of the escapes in this book has you coming back the same route. For instance, you arrive at the Scarborough station on the Hudson Line, hike the aqueduct trail all day, and return from Croton-Harmon.

I will let you know when you should divert from the path to peer through the trees at an octagonal house that resembles a Victorian wedding cake or where to find a comfort station. The really fit may want to scramble up

Breakneck Ridge, while the Sunday walkers may wish to bypass the steep climb yet enjoy the rest of the Hudson Highlands hike. Some outings may spur you on for more, so if a hike from Riverside Park to Spuyten Duyvil isn't long enough, you can continue on north through Riverdale Park.

A few outings warrant spending the night, such as at a Victorian resort along the North Jersey Coast or the utterly charming Hudson River setting of Cold Spring, which offers one of the only inns that directly fronts on the river. My wife, some friends, and I spent a big round birthday at the Hudson House, and we hiked, visited Boscobel Restoration, antiqued, and ate well. Several such places have additional dimensions to explore, or let you simply do nothing and read for the day.

For More Information gives you transportation details as well as telling you about chambers of commerce, eateries, and governmental and nonprofit organizations that provide useful information. The Palisades Interstate Park Commission has a superb Web site; Historic Hudson Valley's site not only tells you all about its properties but also gives links to other places that lie along the routes.

Appendix A, "Hudson Valley Rail Guide," describes what you will see out the train window from Grand Central north to join hikes up Bear Mountain, along the Old Croton Aqueduct Trailway, and deep into the Hudson Highlands.

Appendix B gathers all the useful resources into one place, divided according to categories and geographically. You will find all about what trains, buses, and ferries will carry your bicycle, whether a permit is required (none for the subway), and how much it costs. The New York–New Jersey Trail Conference publishes books, maps, and a newsletter for hikers. Transportation Alternatives does the same for cyclists and pedestrians as well as serving as a lobbying group for bike paths and pedestrian safety.

Go enjoy! We all need to escape, and the out-of-doors may be just an urban hike, a boardwalk bike ride, or a climb into the Highlands away.

—Theodore W. Scull
Manhattan

Key to Icons

 Sailing

 Swimming

 Cycling

 Hiking

 Fishing

 In-line skating

 Kayaking

 Canoeing

 Birding

Manhattan's Wooded West Side North into the Bronx

This is a 10-mile, sometimes undulating hiking and cycling route parallel to the Hudson River, up through two hilly parks and across the Harlem River into the Spuyten Duyvil section of the Bronx.

Itinerary at a Glance

Starting point

Riverside Park, West 72nd Street and Riverside Drive.

Travel directions to starting point

Subway: Broadway #1, #2, #3, or #9 to 72nd Street, and walk 2 blocks west to Riverside Drive.

Bus: M5 to 72nd and Riverside Drive; M57 or M72 to 72nd and West End Avenue, and walk 1 block west; M7 or M11 northbound and M104 to 72nd and Broadway, and walk 2 blocks west; M7 or M11 southbound to 72nd and Columbus Avenue, and walk 3 blocks west.

Car: Limited parking along Riverside Drive and side streets.

Difficulty level and special considerations

This may be one of the most pleasant urban walks and cycling trips in New York City. On the hottest days, it's cool down by the river and in among the trees. The uphills and descents are gentle. There are a number of course changes to keep to the best paths. You can cut the outing short at several different points or even add to the top portion that crosses the Harlem River into the Bronx. Bring a picnic and water, buy lunch at Riverbank State Park (138th through 145th Streets), or buy takeout in the neighborhood just above the George Washington Bridge. Happily, wonderful picnic places abound.

Introduction

The city had great foresight in setting aside existing forests, creating parks, and taking over estates. You can witness all three aspects in this hike and cycle trip along the Hudson River from the south end of Riverside Park to Harlem, north through Fort Washington Park to the George Washington Bridge, up into Fort Tryon Park and Inwood Hill Park and across the Harlem River into the leafy residential Bronx. This outing qualifies as one of the most stimulating forays into natural, created, and architectural New York.

Riverside Park, initially designed in the latter part of the nineteenth century by Frederick Law Olmsted and Charles Vaux of Central Park fame and nurseryman Samuel Parsons, is an absolute treasure and provides the front yard for thousands of West Siders who come down to the linear park and the Hudson to read, take a stroll, jog, and exercise their children and dogs. The parallel, elegant Riverside Drive offers some of the city's best and most attractive residential housing, much of it dating from the 1880s to the 1920s. While the first part of this route sticks to the park, you can shift up to the relatively tranquil drive at almost any point, or make it another day's outing.

Above 125th Street, Harlem's main artery, you cross Riverbank State Park (built atop a sanitation plant), which is laid out with ball fields, jogging tracks, basketball courts, a skating rink, and clusters of benches fronting on the river. Beyond, a very little-known park, remote from the city above, runs north to a red lighthouse that sits under the giant erector set of the George Washington Bridge. When you get to the itinerary, you will learn what generations of city schoolchildren already know: Because of some of their predecessors, the proud little beacon was saved from demolition.

The landscape briefly becomes urban as you climb up into Washington Heights; then, within a few blocks, the neighborhood abruptly changes from busy commercial blocks to pristine apartment complexes and relics of former estates, all sharing million-dollar views of the Hudson's Palisades. The path into Fort Tryon Park leads to a beautiful garden and remnants of battlements designed to keep the British out of New York. (They failed utterly.) A stone tower rises above the trees marking the Cloisters, the medieval wing of the Metropolitan Museum of Art.

The path plunges downward to working-class Inwood at Dyckman Street, then skirts neighborhood ball fields to climb into a real forest at Manhattan's northern tip. For about ten minutes or so, you can be lost in the woods—

The path leads north along the Hudson River to the George Washington Bridge.

until, that is, you arrive alongside the Henry Hudson Bridge tollbooths to take the little-used footpath that shares the busy two-level arch bridge (1936) passing high over the Harlem River to Spuyten Duyvil, a suburban section of the Bronx. There are several diversions, described in the itinerary, but hikers who have had enough can head down to Broadway at West 230th Street for the subway or bus south. Cyclists can use Broadway and St. Nicholas Avenue to enter Central Park at 110th Street.

Itinerary

A statue of Eleanor Roosevelt greets you at the 72nd Street entrance to Riverside Park. Head down past the dog walk and under the Henry Hudson Parkway to the river, where the view opens up south, west, and north. The promenade is open, for cyclists and pedestrians alike, nearly all the way south to the Battery (see Escape 2) and north to 125th Street. The route northward first passes the 79th Street Boat Basin, where there are more permanent residents than visiting yachters living in some pretty rough-and-ready houseboats. It's a private community, so you look in from the shore.

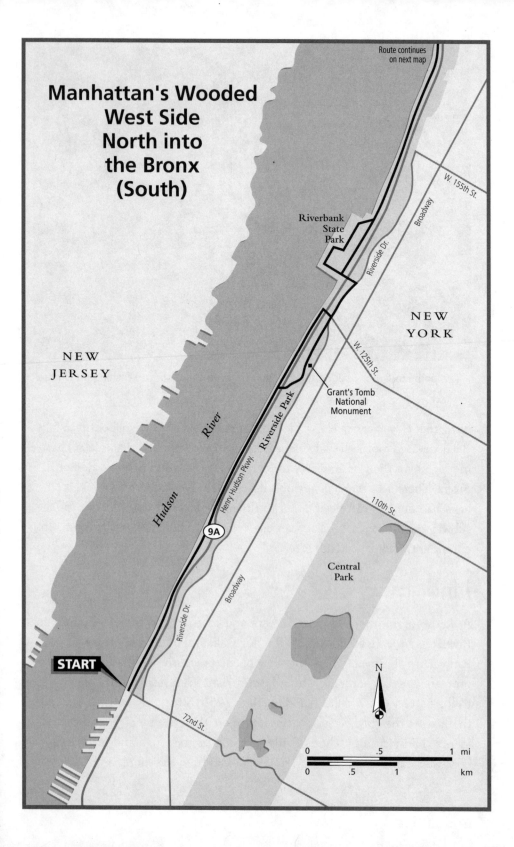

Manhattan's Wooded West Side North into the Bronx (South)

Route continues on next map

W. 155th St.

Riverbank State Park

Broadway

Riverside Dr.

NEW YORK

W. 125th St.

Grant's Tomb National Monument

NEW JERSEY

River

Riverside Park

Hudson

Henry Hudson Pkwy.

110th St.

9A

Central Park

Riverside Dr.

Broadway

START

72nd St.

N

0   .5   1 mi

0   .5   1 km

The path narrows at 86th Street as the parkway curves very close to the river, forcing cyclists briefly inland, though walkers can continue straight ahead. A new paved combination pedestrian-cycling path proceeds for the next 1.5 miles along a narrow strip between the river and the Henry Hudson Parkway to 125th Street.

During this stretch, hikers may choose to shift into Riverside Park on the east side of the parkway and then, at about 120th Street, climb up to Riverside Drive opposite Riverside Church. This imposing interdenominational place of worship and religious activities was financed in the late 1920s by John D. Rockefeller Jr. On a clear day, ride the elevators 355 feet up the tower containing the world's largest carillon and mount the observation deck above that for a terrific view. Riverside Drive now skirts Grant's Tomb, the final resting place for President Ulysses S. and Julia Dent Grant, worth the diversion (free) to have a look within the domed rotunda. The drive passes over a splendid viaduct above 125th Street and then connects at 138th Street with a pedestrian bridge to Riverbank State Park.

The Little Red Lighthouse sits directly under the George Washington Bridge.

Those hikers and cyclists who have remained along the river arrive at the western end of 125th Street to continue north past Fairway, a hugely popular market located beneath the tangle of overhead road and rail structures. Cyclists can proceed on a street-level path to the right of the North River Sanitation Plant to the continuation of a leafy riverside park at 145th Street. Hikers who would like to visit Riverbank State Park, atop the sanitation plant, can climb steps up to 138th Street and cross over a short bridge (no bicycles) to the twenty-two-acre sports facility. There are rest rooms directly ahead, and by walking west to the river, you will come to a peaceful corner with benches to enjoy a pause. Continue north along the riverfront then shift inland past ball fields, a jogging track, a basketball gym, and the indoor roller and ice skating rink. Within this last structure, you will find simple snack facilities, tables,

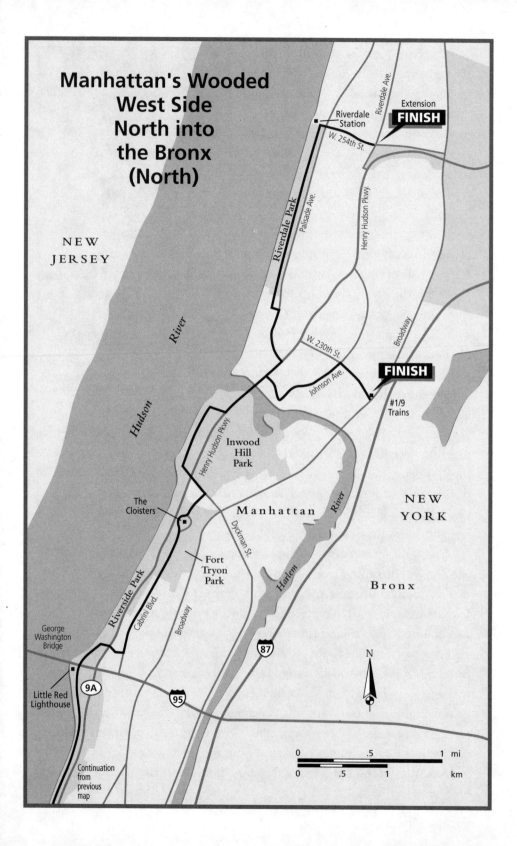

and more rest rooms. Riverbank State Park serves the neighborhood well.

Leave the park at the northeast corner via the stair tower (includes an elevator) to river level and continue northward (with the cyclists) toward the George Washington Bridge. This little-used strip of park is a delight. You pass tennis courts and places to have a picnic on the grass or on benches facing the river. To the right, hidden in the trees, you might see an Amtrak train with passengers sharing the same view along the discreetly placed rail line running north from Penn Station on up the Hudson to Albany and beyond.

Beneath the G. W. Bridge sits a charming red lighthouse, first erected at Sandy Hook, New Jersey, in 1881, then moved here in 1921 to warn ships about the shoals of Jeffrey's Hook. When the bridge opened in 1931, the lighthouse's navigation function was transferred to guiding lights positioned under the bridge span. The beacon was scheduled for demolition until hundreds of the city's children took up the cause after reading the classic *Little Red Lighthouse and the Great Gray Bridge* by Hildegard Hoyt Swift and Lynd Ward. Letters of protest won over the city fathers; the lighthouse is now safe and occasionally opens for tours by the urban park rangers. (See "For More Information," below.)

The path now passes upward under the bridge, loops over the rail tracks, and twists up to a sidewalk alongside the northbound Henry Hudson Parkway. Climb the footbridge over the parkway, turn right past some apartment buildings, and almost immediately turn left up again along West 181st Street to Cabrini Boulevard. This is a mostly Hispanic neighborhood; 1 block higher up, at Fort Washington Avenue, you'll find bodegas if you are in need of refreshments. The George Washington Bridge Bus Station has rest rooms.

Turn left onto Cabrini and you will soon come to two noteworthy apartment complexes—Tudor-style Hudson View Gardens on the right (1924–1925), and to the left the art deco Castle Village (1938–1939), a private and peaceful oasis of lawns and living spaces overlooking the Hudson on the grounds of the former Charles Paterno estate. The neighborhood, while still attractive, becomes more working class until Cabrini Boulevard reaches a plaza and the entrance to Fort Tryon Park. Here the scenic landmark garden is laid out across the former C. K. G. Billings estate. The original stone retaining walls, arches, and drive down to the Henry Hudson Parkway are still visible and worth exploring on foot. Fort Tryon Park is a very special place for locals, and on fine days you will see many older residents enjoying the flower gardens and a seat on one of the raised and recessed benches.

A pre-Revolutionary fort stood here, abandoned by George Washington's troops when the Hessians came south and eventually took New York City. Washington retreated across the Hudson to Fort Lee, the site of another of New York's defenses, and fled on southward. From the raised stone platform in among the trees, look east over Inwood and the Harlem River to the Bronx. As you descend the Cloisters appears as a medieval tower sprouting out of the surrounding woods. The complex houses the Metropolitan Museum's medieval art collection in a series of chapels, rooms, and cloisters that is often filled with the sounds of Renaissance music. There is a fee to enter (free to Metropolitan Museum members).

The park then descends in a switchback fashion to the top end of Riverside Drive as it curves inland to meet Broadway. Cross and continue down to Dyckman Street and turn left toward the river, passing rest rooms on the right. Just beyond the overhead parkway and rail line, turn right into Inwood Hill Park, a flat portion that runs north between the river and a steeply wooded hill. Skirt the ball fields; not quite at the top end, take the prominent footbridge over the tracks and go left into the woods.

The roughly paved path drops then climbs to a fork, the left pathway continuing north for a few more minutes before looping right above the Harlem River and down out of the woods to a well-used water-level park adjacent to the Harlem River. Continue east using West 218th Street past Columbia University's stadium to Broadway, and turn right to reach the elevated 215th Street #1-9 station.

To resume the route to the Bronx, bear right at the fork up a brush-encroaching path to the Henry Hudson Parkway Bridge tolls. The pedestrian-cycle path stays left for a free walk high above the Harlem River, where you look down to the waterway as it passes Amtrak's swing bridge and meets the Hudson. On the Harlem River's north side, Metro-North's tracks join the Hudson River Line just beyond the Spuyten Duyvil station.

Once you're over the bridge on the Bronx side, exit left, then loop back under the parkway along Kappock Street and down to Johnson Avenue. Turn left and downward in the Marble Hill section to West 230th Street, then turn right for the 5 blocks to Broadway. Go either left to the 231st Street #1-9 elevated station or right to the 225th Street station. The subway, with two elevated portions, returns you to your point of departure at 72nd Street and Broadway. For the East Side, board the frequent Bx9 bus south on Broadway, then east to climb through Kingsbridge Heights to the elevated #4 Jerome

Avenue line and to Metro-North's Fordham Road station for Grand Central.

Cyclists can continue south under the el to take the Broadway Bridge into Manhattan, then Broadway to St. Nicholas and the cycle path south to Central Park; or cut west below the George Washington Bridge and take leafy Riverside Drive.

For an extension, after crossing the Harlem River and returning to the street, the Spuyten Duyvil section of leafy residential Riverdale is worth exploring, especially down by the river. Just a block west of the bridge, Henry Hudson Park sports a 100-foot Doric column topped by a bronze statue of Henry Hudson. Palisade Avenue, another block west, runs north into Riverdale, a maze of winding and sometimes poorly maintained streets, to discourage speeding and visiting motorists. At West 232nd Street, go left down into Riverdale Park, a linear ridge that runs north almost continuously for 2 miles above the Metro-North tracks and river. Native American archaeological digs have unearthed signs of settlements dating back 12,000 years. The route is relatively easy to follow and in some places marked. About a mile north, a short diversion uses a parallel road past a few houses before returning to the wooded path. Pass Riverdale Country School and, at the Riverdale station, take the hourly train south to the 125th Street station or Grand Central, or climb the 8 blocks of West 254th Street to Riverdale Avenue. The Bronx bus 7 connects to the #1-9 Broadway Line (elevated here) at West 231st Street. Or you can take the Bx10 that winds through Riverdale, also crosses Broadway at West 231st Street, and continues to the Bedford Park Boulevard station of the #4 Jerome Avenue subway (elevated here) for the East Side.

For More Information

NYC Transit Information: (718) 330–1234; www.mta.info. Subway and bus information.

Metro-North Railroad (Hudson Line): (212) 532–4900 (in New York City); (800) METRO–INFO; www.mta.info.

Riverside Park, Hudson River Park Trust: Pier 40 (foot of West Houston Street and West Street); (917) 661–8740; www.HudsonRiverPark.org.

Riverbank State Park: (212) 694–3600.

Little Red Lighthouse, Inwood Urban Park Rangers: (212) 304–2365. Call for a tour schedule.

The Cloisters: (212) 923–3700; www.metmuseum.org.

This 6-mile combination cycling, hiking, and in-line skating path begins down at the Battery and runs up Manhattan's West Side alongside the Hudson past recreation, ferry, and excursion boat and passenger ship piers into Riverside Park. At Chelsea Piers, outdoor activities include kayaking and sailing.

Itinerary at a Glance

Starting point

Battery Park, Lower Manhattan.

Travel directions to starting point

Subway: #1/9 to South Ferry or #2 to Wall Street; #4 or #5 to Bowling Green; N or R to Whitehall Street.

Bus: M1 (weekdays only) or M6 to Lower Broadway/South Ferry; M15 to South Ferry; M9 or M20 to South End Avenue, Battery Park City.

Ferry: Staten Island Ferry to Whitehall Terminal.

Car: Very limited street parking; otherwise fee parking.

Bicycle: An early start guarantees a more traffic-free ride to the Battery. You can also take your bicycle on the subway. No restrictions.

Difficulty level and special considerations

The waterside route is a level 6-mile, mostly dedicated path for cyclists, skaters, and pedestrians. Some sections that completely separate cyclists and skaters from pedestrians are not yet finished. It is open air; you'll need protection from the sun. Numerous places exist for enjoying views of the river, activities, and food and drink. In spring, summer, and fall, special events often take place, so check the newspapers, Alliance for Downtown New York,

Hudson River Park Trust, and *Time Out New York*. Summer weekends draw lots of people, so be prepared to share the space; if you're cycling, don't expect a fast-track ride. Watch out for turning vehicular traffic in a few places.

Introduction

Probably nowhere in New York has the landscape changed more than along the West Side. This was once the shipping heart of the Port of New York; then containerized cargo handling forced the shipping lines to find more expansive waterfront acreage in Port Elizabeth, Port Newark, and, to a lesser extent, Brooklyn. That sea change opened the waterfront for brand-new uses, and it has taken three long decades for the transformation to mostly recreation.

The overhead West Side Highway is long gone, and a wide new street-level boulevard has taken its place. Between it and the Hudson lie parallel paths with, for many stretches, separated lanes for cycling, skating, and hiking, so this chapter covers a most pleasant down-by-the-riverside outing. The Hudson River Park path will eventually extend all the way to the Adirondacks, and segments farther north are already in place. Escape 1 in the previous chapter, for example, takes you from Riverside Park up past the George Washington Bridge into the Riverdale section of the Bronx. Escapes 17 and 18 cross the George Washington Bridge to parallel the New Jersey Palisades.

If you're cycling, this is not a high-speed route but a sight-seeing one; it's worth slowing down to take in the grand city planning at Battery Park City and what will eventually rise at the former World Trade Center site. Be sure to stop to explore the Chelsea recreation pier complex and pause at the USS *Intrepid* Sea-Air-Space Museum, if only to look up at the World War II aircraft carrier looming overhead. If it's a May-through-October weekend, cruise ships will be berthed at the Passenger Ship Terminal in the West 50s. Finally, glide north along a new link into Riverside Park, one of New York City's real treasures.

Hudson River Park, the overall name for the route you will follow, is a work in progress, and as it expands and matures, it will only get better.

Itinerary

The Battery is many things—a park; a setting for sculpture and memorials; the landing for Ellis Island, the Statue of Liberty, and NY Waterway ferries to

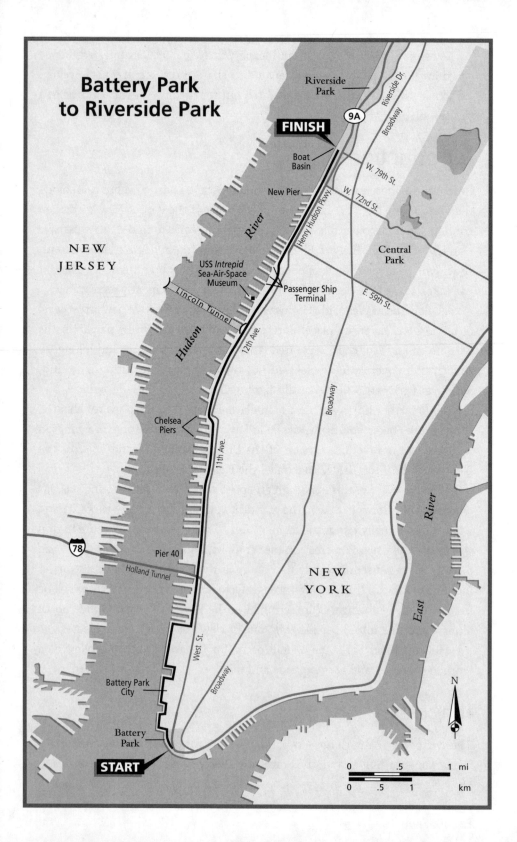

Battery Park
to Riverside Park

Riverside
Park

9A

FINISH

Boat
Basin

New Pier

W. 79th St.

W. 72nd St.

NEW
JERSEY

River

Central
Park

USS *Intrepid*
Sea-Air-Space
Museum

Passenger Ship
Terminal

E. 59th St.

Lincoln Tunnel

Hudson

12th Ave.

Henry Hudson Pkwy.

Broadway

Riverside Dr.

Broadway

Chelsea
Piers

11th Ave.

River

78

Pier 40

Holland Tunnel

NEW
YORK

East

West St.

Battery Park
City

Broadway

N

Battery
Park

START

0   .5   1 mi

0   .5   1   km

New Jersey; and the location for an early-nineteenth-century fort. The immediate surroundings include Upper New York Bay, the Staten Island Ferry Terminal, a wonderful former fireboat pier, the merchant marine war memorial, some fine office buildings, and the Museum of the American Indian, housed in the old Beaux Arts Custom House.

The riverside path begins at Robert F. Wagner Jr. Park, a grassy lawn with a raised viewing platform for eyeing the harbor traffic. The Museum of Jewish Heritage is also here, and adjacent to it you will see some whimsical sculpture. The original Manhattan Island littoral is re-created at South Cove with the waves lapping at boulders and beach grass; above here, the route becomes a fine tree-lined esplanade located where banana-handling piers used to jut into the river. Battery Park City shows off how attractive a multipurpose residential and office complex can be, and the architecture is a nice blending of materials and varying heights. Wouldn't it be nice to have a wee pied-à-terre here?

The route skirts North Cove, home for fancy yachts and charter craft, and at the top end, the NY Waterway ferry crosses to Jersey City and Hoboken. My wife and I had our wedding reception one flight up at the Hudson River Club on the north side of North Cove after being married in St. Paul's Chapel 3 blocks to the east.

The esplanade continues straight north past a beautifully designed children's playground, an undulating grassy lawn, and a whimsical sculpture park before turning sharp right then sharp left to follow the bulkhead and designated biking, skating, and hiking paths. Along this stretch there are recreation piers, with all sorts of activities taking place.

Pier 40, a square rather than finger-shaped pier, was designed in the early 1960s to handle the emerging container trade as well as Holland America Line's passenger fleet, and the pier now serves as a parking lot and recreation center. Before reaching the Chelsea Pier complex, you come to a lone steel arch that framed the Pier 54 head house used by Cunard and later Cunard–White Star Line. The *Carpathia* arrived here with the *Titanic's* survivors in April 1912, and the *Lusitania* sailed from here in May 1915 to be torpedoed by a German U-boat off Ireland a few days later.

You can pass directly in front of the Chelsea Piers or take the more interesting pier path that skirts a caged golf driving range and then goes under cover along the complex's river-facing gallery. Within are rock climbing walls, gymnastics, soccer, figure skating, basketball courts, and other facilities that draw adults, families who want to play together, and even birthday party gatherings. Note the large black-and-white photo murals that show the Chelsea Piers when they served ships, with scenes of these once magnificent structures under construction; film stars, troops, and Olympic athletes arriving home; and longshoremen attending a worship service. The *Titanic* should have arrived at Pier 61 in April 1912. In addition, you'll find a delicatessen, cafe, restaurant, drinking fountain, and rest room facilities.

At Piers 62 and 63, the Offshore Sailing School offers three-day courses, and kayaks can be rented at the Manhattan Kayak Company (see "For More Information," below). Hockey, in-line skating, and skateboarding take place; or inspect a 1933 New York City fireboat, the *John J. Harvey*, the lightship *Frying Pan*, and tugboat *Bertha*.

The path runs straight again past some architecturally significant recycled warehouses from the immediate post–Civil War period to the 1930s, a sightseeing heliport, the black-glass Jacob Javits Convention Center, former United States Lines cargo-container piers, the NY Waterway ferry terminal to Weehawken, Lincoln Harbor, and Hoboken, the Circle Line (sight-seeing) and World Yacht (dinner boats) piers, and the USS *Intrepid* Sea-Air-Space Museum. The three piers (88, 90, and 92) make up the Passenger Ship Terminal, which hums with activity every weekend from May into October and some weekdays. One of the delights is to stand beneath the bow of the *Queen Elizabeth 2* or *Queen Mary 2* then watch her slip her lines and reverse into the river to begin her fast six-day crossing to England. (See "For More Information" for ship sailing information.)

Above the ship terminal, the path enters Riverside South, located partly beneath the overhead Henry Hudson Parkway. The huge apartment complex, belonging to Donald Trump, has injected thousands of new residents into what was once railroad marshaling yards. Remains of former New York Central car-float transfer piers are to the left. A new finger pier angles southwest into the river and is a terrific viewpoint up, down, and across the Hudson. At 72nd Street, you enter the south end of Riverside Park, which extends to 125th Street then, with brief interruptions, returns as a park up to and under the George Washington Bridge.

Riverside Park is the favored by West Side residents for walking their dogs, taking their children to a playground, sitting on a bench reading, or jogging. Rest room facilities are located just below the 79th Street Boat Basin.

Riverside Park is a gem of city planning, as are Riverside Drive and the lovely undulating line of town houses and apartment buildings that run

The combination cycle and pedestrian path runs north-south through Riverside Park on Manhattan's West Side.

continuously for almost 3 miles, punctuated by the Soldiers' and Sailors' Monument, Grant's Tomb, and Riverside Church. Frederick Law Olmsted and Charles Vaux designed Riverside Park, though it was later altered to make room for the Henry Hudson Parkway, which is largely masked from sight and sound—but reduces the park to a very narrow path.

Hikers can walk to 125th Street, and cyclists detour inland at 86th Street then return to a new bike-pedestrian path to continue north. The previous chapter (Escape 1) describes the hike and cycle route from Riverside Park to Spuyten Duyvil in the Bronx. Go for it.

For More Information

New York City Transit Authority: (718) 330–1234; www.mta.info. Subway and bus information.

Alliance for Downtown New York: (212) 566–6700; www.downtownny.com.

Battery Park City Authority: (212) 417–2000; www.batteryparkcity.org.

Hudson River Park Trust: Pier 40 (foot of West Houston Street and West Street); (917) 661–8740; www.HudsonRiverPark.org.

Metropolitan Waterfront Alliance: 457 Madison Avenue, New York, NY 10022; (800) 364–9943; www.waterwire.net.

Museum of Jewish Heritage: (212) 509–6130; www.mjhnyc.org.

New York Waterway: (800) 53–FERRY; www.nywaterway.com.

Chelsea Piers Sports and Entertainment Complex: 23rd Street and the Hudson, New York, NY 10011; (212) 336–6800; www.chelseapiers.com.

Manhattan Kayak Company Pier 63: (212) 924–1788; www.manhattan kayak.com.

Offshore Sailing School: Chelsea Piers; (800) 221–4326; www.offshore sailing.com.

Intrepid *Sea-Air-Space Museum:* (212) 245–0072; www.intrepidmuseum.com.

Passenger Ship Terminal: www.nypst.com (ship arrivals and departures); www.worldshipny.com (World Ship Society site for arrivals and departures).

3 Broadway from the Battery to the Bronx

This ultimate urban hike begins near the southern tip of Manhattan and angles north for 18 miles, threading the entire length of the island and part of the Bronx, through every kind of New York neighborhood, to the Yonkers city line.

Itinerary at a Glance

Starting point

Opposite No. 1 Broadway on the steps of the Alexander Hamilton Custom House.

Travel directions to starting point

Subway: #1/9 to South Ferry; #4 or #5 to Bowling Green; N or R to Whitehall Street.

Bus: M1 (weekdays only) or M6 to Lower Broadway; M15 to South Ferry; M9 or M20 to South End Avenue, Battery Park City.

Ferry: Staten Island Ferry to Whitehall Terminal.

Car: Very limited street parking; otherwise, fee parking.

Difficulty level and special considerations

This mostly level 18-mile walk is all on pavement, but the urban stimulation should keep you going to the rewarding end. One key to enjoying the day is finding the right pace to avoid stopping at street corners because of crossing traffic and traffic lights. If you begin early, traffic interference will be minimal—except at major cross streets—until about Herald Square. Then it's busy with crossing traffic until the side streets in West Harlem. Also, start early enough to avoid arriving in Yonkers after dark. If you set out by 8:30 A.M. and allow one-hour-plus for stops along the way, steady walkers should reach Yonkers by 5:00 P.M. (with some lingering to sight-see). Rest room stops are available along the way at hotels, large stores, and the big-chain fast-food outlets.

Introduction

There is no question about it: Walking Broadway from the Battery north to the Bronx is the ultimate urban walk. The kaleidoscope of neighborhoods—commercial, residential, entertainment—through which you will pass will spur you on to the very end. Walkers I have known have begun the day thinking that they will not last it out, then ended up doing the whole route, because the sensorial stimulation is that powerful.

The Broadway alignment as we know it today is generally considered to have started out as a Native American ridge trail that ran the length of what we now call Manhattan Island and into the present-day Bronx. The name *Broadway* continues beyond New York City into Westchester County, so you will encounter it again if you take the Old Croton Aqueduct Trailway hike (see Escape 12).

Broadway officially starts at No. 1, in the former steamship line office district opposite the Beaux Arts former U.S. Custom House. It heads north past Bowling Green, which once was one but now is a little triangular park with a bronze "Wall Street" bull at the top end. The initial sites are in the financial district, with some splendid architecture, a couple of historic churches—Trinity and St. Paul's—and City Hall, with its beautifully made-over park.

The neighborhoods change quickly from Tribeca (triangle below Canal) and Soho (south of Houston), with their fine industrial architecture and now lively street life, to the even more animated and varied inhabitants and visitors encountered in Greenwich Village. Then it's on past Union Square, the completely revamped Madison Square Park, and the Middle Eastern bazaar trade to Herald Square, the traditional department store district anchored now by Macy's.

Times Square is likely to be reasonably quiet early in the day, and then it's on to the Columbus Circle area, where you get your only glimpse of Central Park. You have now arrived in the Upper West Side, which extends from 59th Street well up to Columbia University and on into Spanish Harlem, where there is a complete cultural change and lots of active street life by midafternoon.

At the very top of the island, cross the Harlem River into the Bronx, walking beneath the #1/9 Broadway elevated line that will remain your roof until it comes to an abrupt end at 242nd Street. You end the day walking alongside Van Cortlandt Park up into Yonkers, one of New York State's largest cities, though its boundary with New York City may seem rather blurry until you see the sign and enjoy a sigh of relief.

The triangular Flatiron Building, arguably Manhattan's first skyscraper, is located where Broadway crosses Fifth Avenue at 23rd Street.

Itinerary

If you have done your homework with a bit of reading about Broadway or already know stretches of it, then stand on the steps of the former U.S. Custom House with your eyes closed and imagine the neighborhoods, parks, and sights you are about to see during the long and stimulating day ahead.

The statues on either side of you represent four continents, but not South America, Australia, or Antarctica. They represent a view of the world just after 1900, and it's not a politically correct view by today's standards. When U.S. Customs moved to 7 World Trade Center (now destroyed) in the early 1970s, the opulent original building stayed dark until the Museum of the American Indian moved in. It's free, but you may arrive too early in the day for a visit. Across the street is No. 1 Broadway, the former headquarters for United States Lines; on the south-facing facade, you can see shields representing world port destinations and two doors that led into the old booking hall marked FIRST CLASS and CABIN CLASS.

There is still a bit of Manhattan to the south—Battery Park, Castle Clinton, and the Staten Island Ferry Terminal. At the beginning of the walk, I prefer the west side of Broadway, most of the way north to Yonkers. It's much livelier, though you may find reasons to cross over from time to time to take in a park or square.

The mighty Cunard Line had its own building at 25 Broadway, now a post office, and other steamship lines occupied many more buildings from here up to Trinity Church (1846) at the head of Wall Street. Trinity is worth poking your head inside, as is the even older and very different St. Paul's Chapel (1764–1766), if it's open. Opposite the south end of City Hall Park is the Woolworth Building (1913) with a magnificent lobby; framing the east side of City Hall Park is the former newspaper row that followed city politics unfolding inside City Hall (1802–1812).

The neighborhood changes character to low-rise and older buildings as Broadway leaves Lower Manhattan and enters Tribeca and Soho, once the industrial heart of Manhattan and now largely recycled into residential lofts, apartments, stores, restaurants, and markets. There are a couple of major streets to cross—Canal and Houston—that will break your pace. The numbered streets begin above Houston with 1st and continue up to 263rd, but don't look at each sign or you may never make it. Greenwich Village, both pleasant and somewhat ragtag, will be relatively tranquil in the morning. The

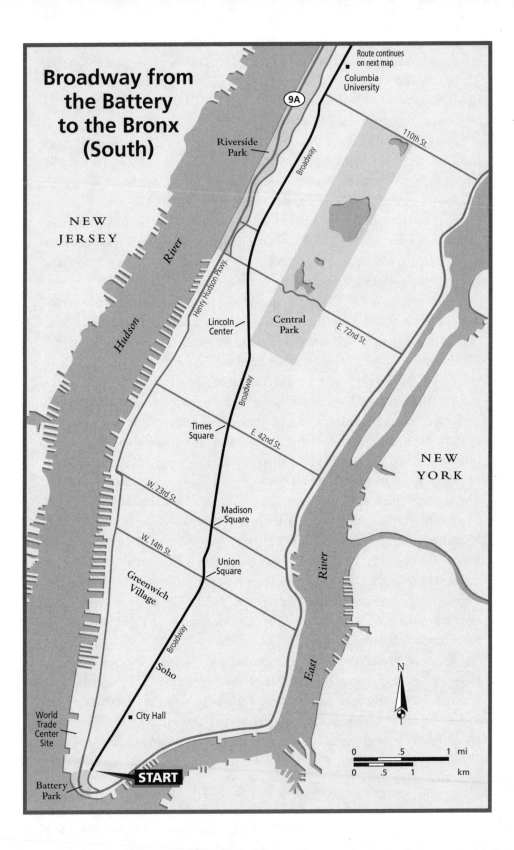

Broadway from the Battery to the Bronx (South)

Route continues on next map

Columbia University

9A

Riverside Park

110th St.

NEW JERSEY

Hudson River

Broadway

Central Park

Henry Hudson Pkwy.

Lincoln Center

E. 72nd St.

Broadway

Times Square

E. 42nd St.

NEW YORK

W. 23rd St.

Madison Square

W. 14th St.

Union Square

Greenwich Village

East River

Broadway

Soho

City Hall

N

World Trade Center Site

START

Battery Park

| 0 | .5 | 1 mi |
| 0 | .5 | 1 km |

street grid does not begin in earnest until 14th Street, where you encounter the lively and very popular Union Square Market, followed by a most attractive relandscaping of Madison Square Park above 23rd Street. Spin around at 23rd to see the triangular Flatiron Building.

The tiny retail shops along the next stretch to Herald Square make you think you are in the Middle East, and then bang, you pass Macy's, the world's largest department store. It's on through the garment district to 42nd Street and Times Square, the country's burgeoning entertainment center, which has seen a heavy dose of Disney style added to its traditional theaters, porn, and illuminated advertising signs. The Marriott Marquis is a very good place to spend a penny, with rest rooms on many of the conference floors starting just above street level. Use the escalators.

At Columbus Circle, the AOL Time Warner Center contains offices, television studios, theaters for Jazz at Lincoln Center, a Mandarin Oriental Hotel, restaurants, luxury apartments, and retail stores in a new fifty-five-story, 750-foot twin-tower complex that replaced the Coliseum. Columbus Circle is also Mile 0 for the old post roads radiating from the city.

The Upper West Side, one of the city's most energetic and prized neighborhoods, begins in earnest above Lincoln Center with a wonderful cityscape of turn-of-the-twentieth-century Beaux Arts apartment houses, lots of restaurants, and some of the best shopping in the city, especially for food, at Fairway, Citarella, and Zabar's, the latter the ultimate (madhouse) of all delis. There is a tiny park at 106th Street dedicated to Isador and Isaac Straus (R. H. Macy owner), the couple who drowned together when the *Titanic* sank in 1912. The bustling character holds until about 96th Street, then quiets down until you cross 110th, where Broadway becomes Columbia University's main street. Think about having lunch now, with so many inexpensive restaurants representing many nationalities lining these blocks. Or if you brought food, walk down the hill a block to Riverside Drive and rest for a bit in leafy, peaceful surroundings.

As Broadway descends from Columbia, you will see another dramatic change when you approach 125th Street and Spanish (West) Harlem. You'll then climb again through as much street life as seen in the Upper West Side in the 70s and 80s, though culturally it's very different. By 168th Street, you are in New York Presbyterian Hospital country. Then Broadway skirts the hulk of the George Washington Bridge Bus Station (rest rooms), and you sense you are entering a valley.

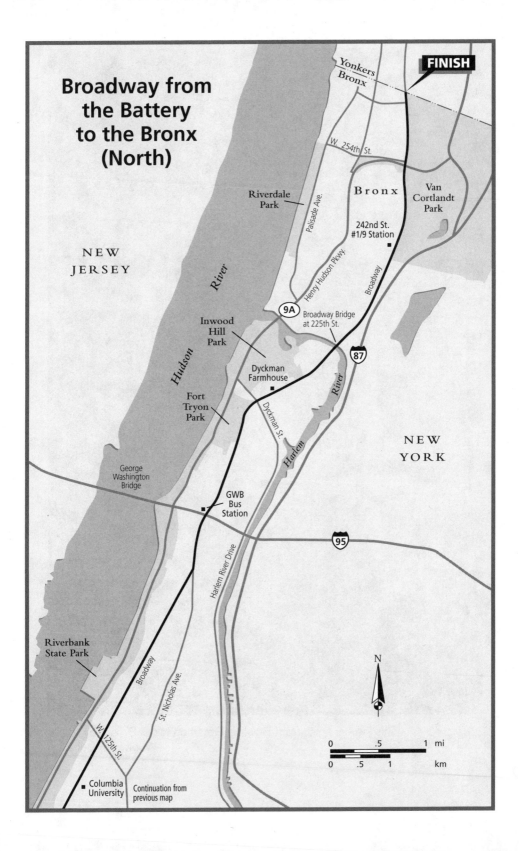

Broadway from the Battery to the Bronx (North)

FINISH

Yonkers
Bronx

W. 254th St.

Bronx

Riverdale
Park

Palisade Ave.

Van
Cortlandt
Park

242nd St.
#1/9 Station

NEW
JERSEY

Hudson River

Henry Hudson Pkwy.

Broadway

9A

Inwood
Hill
Park

Broadway Bridge
at 225th St.

87

Dyckman
Farmhouse

Harlem River

Fort
Tryon
Park

Dyckman St.

NEW
YORK

Hudson River

Harlem

George
Washington
Bridge

GWB
Bus
Station

95

Harlem River Drive

N

Riverbank
State Park

Broadway

St. Nicholas Ave.

W. 125th St.

Columbia
University

Continuation from
previous map

| 0 | .5 | 1 mi |
| 0 | .5 | 1 km |

This view is north from Bowling Green on lower Broadway to the
Woolworth Building.

Passing alongside Fort Tryon Park, which rises to the left at West 204th Street, you will be amazed to see a Dutch-style farmhouse sandwiched into a lot that is surrounded by old low-rise apartment houses. Rebuilt after the Revolution in 1783, the Dyckman Farmhouse Museum is the last residential farm building in Manhattan, and it may be open as you pass.

While crossing the Harlem River via the Broadway Bridge—which carries a footpath, vehicular traffic, and an elevated subway line—look west along the river to the Hudson and the beautiful New Jersey Palisades. A later chapter (Escape 18) outlines the hike across the river. Once you're in the Bronx at 225th Street, the elevated overhead railway remains a noisy shelter until 242nd Street. Here, cross over to the Van Cortlandt Park side (rest rooms) for the final, and unfortunately dull, stretch to Yonkers, the city line beginning at the top of the hill. A wooden welcome sign will tell you have arrived—congratulations! Pat everyone on the back, and treat yourselves to the bus back to the subway! The Bronx bus Bx9 starts just inside the New York City limits and connects to the #1/9, #4, D, #2, and #5 subway lines and Metro-North's Fordham Road station, so you can reach Manhattan's East and West Sides.

For More Information

New York City Transit Authority: (718) 330–1234; www.mta.info. Subway and bus information.

Dyckman Farmhouse Museum: (212) 304–9422. Historic House Trust of New York City: (212) 360–8282; www.nyc.gov/parks or www.preserve.org/hht.

4 Five Bridges and Three Boroughs

This highly creative 9-mile, semi-aerial hike and cycle route crosses the East River via the Queensboro, Williamsburg, Manhattan, and Brooklyn Bridges and between Queens and Brooklyn via the Pulaski Bridge. The bridges themselves provide more than half the total mileage!

Itinerary at a Glance

Starting point

First Avenue and East 60th Street, Manhattan.

Travel directions to starting point

Subway: N, R, or W to 59th Street and Lexington Avenue; exit to Third Avenue and walk east on 60th Street. F to 63rd Street and Lexington Avenue. Or take the #4, #5, or #6 to 59th Street and Lexington Avenue.

Bus: M15 south on Second Avenue to 60th Street. M15 north on First Avenue to 60th Street. M101, M102, M103 south on Lexington to 60th. M101, M102, M103 north on Third to 60th. Q32 from Penn Station up Madison and across 59th Street to Second Avenue; walk 1 block north, then east. M31 or M57 east on 57th Street to First Avenue, and walk 3 blocks north under the Queensboro Bridge approach.

Car: Park on the street if possible, otherwise in a garage. To return to your car from City Hall, Manhattan, take the Lexington Avenue express #4 or #5 subway from Brooklyn Bridge/City Hall to 59th Street, or the M103 bus from Park Row/City Hall up Third Avenue to 60th Street.

Difficulty level and special considerations

These 9 miles are almost entirely flat, though there are steps up to and down from some of the bridge paths. The maximum is seventy-four for the Pulaski Bridge. Cyclists can avoid this last one as described in the itinerary section. None of the bridges should worry anyone with mild acrophobia or vertigo, because the walkways have reassuring railing protection. While cyclists and hikers have separate lanes, you need to watch out for aggressive riders, especially regular users on the Brooklyn Bridge. It's always wise to stay in your lane and cross into the bike lane only after looking very carefully. Improvements to the walkways on the Manhattan and Williamsburg Bridges are ongoing long-term projects.

Introduction

The bridges of New York have always provided some of the best viewing platforms in the city. All, except for the Verrazano-Narrows Bridge, have combination walkways and cycle paths. Manhattan, as it is an island, has bridges crossing the Hudson, East, and Harlem Rivers. Many are architecturally interesting structures with diverse styles—suspension, cantilever, arch, bascule, draw, swing, and lift span.

For this hike, the four East River bridges make for a great outing. At either end, there are neighborhoods to explore, such as Polish Greenpoint, arty and Hasidic Williamsburg, and the melting pot of the Lower East Side.

In order, they are the Queensboro Bridge from the Upper East Side, with great views north up the East River, down to Roosevelt Island, and across to Long Island City, Queens. The itinerary continues down to the East River for an exploratory waterfront route to the Pulaski Bridge over Newtown Creek into Greenpoint, Brooklyn.

The longest city street stretch passes along this strongly Hispanic then Polish commercial hub into Williamsburg, which is a new art colony, then into black and Hasidic neighborhoods. Cross the Williamsburg Bridge, sharing the span between the adjacent subway line and the vehicle lanes across to Delancey Street, a major artery that meets Orchard Street, the heart of the Lower East Side bargain shopping district. Pass through a corner of Chinatown to the Manhattan Bridge, to cross from the Bowery over to Brooklyn in the midst of the Jehovah's Witnesses' headquarters. It's a short 0.3 mile to the Brooklyn Bridge approach, and you end the day with the best

This hiker looks across from Long Island City to the East Side of Manhattan and the United Nations, Tudor City, and the Chrysler Building.

views of all, including Lower Manhattan and much of New York Harbor.

Itinerary

From First Avenue, a bike-pedestrian lane alongside the Queensboro Bridge approach parallels 60th Street up toward Second Avenue, then turns a tight 180 degrees to the bridge itself. The walkway parallels the westbound roadway on the right and the Roosevelt Island Tramway dangling by to the left. You first cross the East River's main channel, with the entire Upper East Side from New York Presbyterian Hospital to the mayor's Gracie Mansion stretching away below you. The Queensboro Bridge, completed in 1909, is a decorative cantilever span with a maximum clearance of 135 feet above the East River at mean high water.

The parallel tramway drops down to Roosevelt Island; the view from the bridge is northward to the new Southtown complex, earlier residential sections, and Bird S. Coler Memorial Hospital. Formerly Welfare Island, this East

River island was once all hospital and psychiatric facilities. The outer roadway you use had a trolley line, and at the midway point, a stop served an elevator that descended to the island, carrying vehicles until 1955 and pedestrians to 1975. After crossing the East Channel, the walkway drops past the N subway tracks to the street at Queensboro Plaza.

Double back 5 blocks to Vernon Boulevard and turn left past the old New York Architectural Terra-Cotta Company office (1892), with its terra-cotta trim and gabled roof. Passing the Fila sports center on the right, you come to 46th Avenue and turn right toward the backside of the giant Pepsi-Cola sign (1936). At the bottling plant, turn left, continue to 48th Avenue, and turn right past Citilights, a new high-rise apartment complex. Recreation piers jut into the East River on either side of the former Long Island Rail Road gantries that used to transfer rail freight cars from barges to the tracks that connected to the LIRR branches.

You will find rest room facilities and, at the end of the southernmost pier, benches and fish-cleaning tables. The view across to Manhattan includes the United Nations, Beekman Place, and Tudor City. Walk inland and turn right past the McKim, Meade and White–designed power plant (1939) that once generated electricity for both the Pennsylvania Railroad and Long Island Rail Road. Overlapping PRR and LIRR lettering can be seen in the metal sewer covers. Have a look inside the Waterfront Crab House at the jumble of memorabilia, and at this corner turn left and go around the Queens Midtown Tunnel ventilation shaft (1939). Follow Borden Avenue between the tunnel approach and the LIRR yards.

At 11th Street, turn right, cross the tracks, and climb the seventy-four-step tower to the Pulaski Bridge (bascule, 1954). This lift span crosses Newtown Creek, an industrial waterway that winds several miles inland and forms the boundary between Queens and Brooklyn. Use the stair tower at the Brooklyn end down to the street. Cyclists can double back a couple of blocks to the ramped walkway across the Pulaski Bridge, continue to street level, then turn right 1 block and left onto Manhattan Avenue. Hikers at street level can continue in the same direction and turn right onto Clay Street, then left onto Manhattan. The largely Hispanic neighborhood becomes increasingly active and changes to a mostly Polish community, as evidenced by signs in many store windows. The few blocks on either side of the imposing St. Anthony of Padua Roman Catholic Church form the commercial hub, with inexpensive restaurants for a meal of hot or cold borscht, cheese or meat pierogi, kielbasa, sauerkraut,

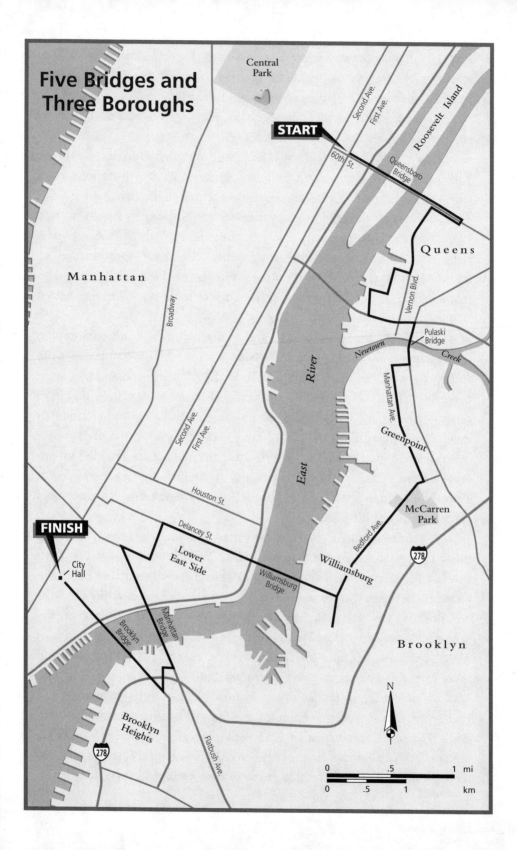

Five Bridges and
Three Boroughs

Central
Park

START

Second Ave.

First Ave.

60th St.

Queensboro
Bridge

Roosevelt Island

Queens

Manhattan

Broadway

Vernon Blvd.

Pulaski
Bridge

Newtown   Creek

Second Ave.

First Ave.

East   River

Manhattan Ave.

Greenpoint

Houston St.

McCarren
Park

FINISH

Delancey St.

City
Hall

Lower
East Side

Bedford Ave.

278

Williamsburg
Bridge

Williamsburg

Manhattan
Bridge

Brooklyn
Bridge

Brooklyn

N

Brooklyn
Heights

278

Flatbush Ave.

0   .5   1   mi

0   .5   1   km

and potato pancakes. From the church steps, the Greenpoint Historic District, made up of churches, banks, and row houses, centers on Milton (ahead) and immediately parallel streets; it's worth a zigzag.

Continue south along Manhattan Avenue to turn right onto Nassau Avenue, then immediately bear left onto Bedford Street through McCarren Park into Williamsburg. Bedford becomes increasingly busy again as it enters an emerging artists colony, mostly young people who cannot afford more expensive Park Slope or Greenwich Village. For several blocks, small cafes and shops line the street; once you're past Metropolitan Avenue, the impressive City Baths (1922), an indoor swimming pool, lies within a brick building on the left. Bedford becomes a mostly Hispanic neighborhood for the remaining blocks to the Williamsburg Bridge overpass, where the bridge pathway heads right and gradually up the span.

As a diversion, continue across Broadway and follow Bedford to the Hasidic neighborhood that begins in earnest beyond Division Avenue. These Jews, with their distinctive clothing and hairstyle, came to Brooklyn from Eastern Europe in the years following World War II; large numbers also arrived more recently. A short loop of a few blocks takes you back to Broadway. At No. 178, Peter Luger's has served some of the best steaks in New York since the late nineteenth century.

The Williamsburg Bridge (suspension, 1903) has its path on the south side, looking toward the former Brooklyn Navy Yard—now a ship repair facility and industrial park—and to the Manhattan and Brooklyn Bridges. The J and M subway lines parallel the path that at the Manhattan end shifts left to a set of steps leading down into the very busy Lower East Side along Delancey Street. You might wish to cross to Delancey's more vibrant north side. Both McDonald's and Burger King have rest rooms.

At Orchard Street, the main shopping blocks run north, but to reach the Manhattan Bridge (suspension, 1909), turn left (south) past the Tenement Museum, where you can learn about generations of families who occupied one building furnished in early immigrants' style. At Canal Street, turn right and cross wide Allen Street, continuing up to the Bowery—a busy junction of streets with a domed former bank building on the southwest corner. The safest way to reach the bridge path, located on the Manhattan Bridge's south side, is to cross the Bowery, go left across Canal then left again across the Bowery, and cross the bridge approach to the path that skirts the monumental arched bridge entrance. This pathway was closed from about 1960 to 2001 and remains a bit of a secret to most New Yorkers.

The bridge path is sandwiched between the Q and W train subway tracks; a caged railing with great views of the Brooklyn Bridge is not far away. The first stretch passes above Division Street and East Broadway, teeming commercial blocks in the heart of Chinatown that carry the eye to looming backdrop of the modern skyscrapers of Lower Manhattan—now missing the twin towers of the World Trade Center.

At the Brooklyn end, go 180 degrees around to the right and follow Jay Street under the bridge approach. Turn left onto wide Prospect Street, head under another approach turn left up to Cadman Plaza East, which runs beneath the Brooklyn Bridge approach. It's more obvious than it sounds. A short set of steps leads right up to the bridge walkway. If you continue ahead, you come to Cadman Plaza, a leafy park with drinking fountain and benches that divides Brooklyn Heights from downtown Brooklyn, and another walk.

The Brooklyn Bridge (suspension, 1883) pathway is in all the tourist guides, so you will hear languages from around the world. The pedestrian path is to the left, and it cannot be said too often: Watch for high-speed cyclists on the right. There will be times, especially at the two stone towers, that you will want to cross over to the north side to look at the view of Midtown Manhattan or to read the historical plaques. Be certain to look both ways.

The view takes in Brooklyn Heights, the docks below the Heights, Governors Island—behind which lies Upper New York Bay, Staten Island, and the Verrazano-Narrows Bridge at the harbor entrance—and all of Lower Manhattan and South Street Seaport. It's a fine feast for the eye. When completed in 1883, this walkway qualified as the world's highest human-built viewing point. It may have been long since surpassed in height, but nothing can take away from the interest all around you.

The walkway slopes down past Pace University to the left and the New York City Police Department headquarters and criminal court buildings to the right, with the tall (wedding cake) Municipal Building and tiny City Hall directly ahead. At the bottom end, you can cross into City Hall Park and look back at the way you came.

To return uptown, cyclists have dedicated bike lane stretches on Centre Street, then on Lafayette Street above Grand, Fourth Avenue to Union Square, Broadway to Columbus Circle, and on up Central Park West. East Siders can use Central Park itself to continue north. The #4, #5, or #6 City Hall/Brooklyn Bridge subway station entrance is here; or for the #2 or #3 West Side Line,

The Brooklyn Bridge has had a popular walkway since it opened in May 1883.

cross the park in front of City Hall to Park Place leading off Broadway. For the N or R, cross the park to Broadway. City Hall Park itself is a great place to have a seat and contemplate the wonderful day.

For More Information

New York City Transit Authority: (718) 330–1234; www.mta.info. Subway and bus information.

Brooklyn Bridge: www.nyctourist.com/bridge1.htm.

Brooklyn Information & Culture: www.brooklynX.org or www.brooklynonline.com. Information on Greenpoint and Williamsburg.

Peter Luger Steak House, 178 Broadway: (718) 387–7400; www.peterluger.com. Cash only, no credit cards.

5 Crossing the Bronx: Pelham Bay Park to Upper Manhattan

This is an ethnically and geographically diverse 8- to 10-mile walk across the Bronx from Pelham Bay Park through Bronx Park, Belmont, Fordham, and University Heights, then down into Upper Manhattan.

Itinerary at a Glance

Starting point

Pelham Bay station, #6 train, northeast Bronx.

Travel directions to starting point

Subway: Lexington Avenue Local, #6 train, from stations on the East Side to the end of the line at Pelham Bay Park.

Car: Bruckner Expressway (I–95) north to Pelham Parkway. Park on the street near the subway (elevated) terminal. The frequent Bx12 bus returns here directly from Upper Manhattan at the end of the day.

Difficulty level and special considerations

The hike is mostly level apart from a climb along Fordham Road to University Heights and the drop down to the Harlem River. There are a number of suggested diversions that, if taken, can add considerable interest to the direct route across the borough. Five hours on foot (not including travel time to the starting point), with an hour for lunch and a couple of diversions, would be the minimum time frame. Allow up to eight hours if you're routing through the New York Botanical Garden. Public rest room facilities are few, and these will be noted. Irritatingly, some of the nationwide fast-food chains that normally offer rest rooms do not necessarily either have them or keep them in proper working order. Taking a picnic is superfluous—eateries for every imaginable taste

The New York Botanical Garden makes a tranquil addition
to a walk across the Bronx.

cluster under the els and along Italian Arthur Avenue and the Fordham
Road commercial strip. The very interesting indoor Arthur Avenue Retail
Market is not generally open on Sunday, so Saturday is a better day.

Introduction

The borough of the Bronx is as diverse as Brooklyn, and for many can be the
most puzzling in terms of where to go, apart from the Bronx Zoo and the New
York Botanical Garden.

From the northeast Bronx at Pelham Bay Park then westward across the
borough, there are intensely distinctive neighborhoods that are both suburban and urban, middle class and largely Caucasian, heavily Hispanic, Italian,
Irish, and African American. Pelham Parkway and Fordham Road cross every
north–south subway line, some elevated and others underground, and the
intersections provide thriving commercial strips catering to the adjoining
neighborhoods.

By straying occasionally from the east–west track, you'll find architectural gems, curiosities, and intensely ethnic neighborhoods such as Arthur Avenue and side streets in the Italian Belmont section. A detour through the New York Botanical Garden is easy to add, while a visit to the Bronx Zoo should be considered a separate outing. In the University Heights section, Fordham Road crosses the old Croton Aqueduct, and the distinctive pathway atop the rounded structure might spur you to exploring its entire length deep into rural wooded Westchester County (see Escape 12).

The cross-Bronx hike ends by winding down to the Harlem River, crossing on a nineteenth-century swing bridge, and returning south via the West Side #1/9 train or the M100 bus along Broadway.

Itinerary

The subway ride (about forty-five minutes from 86th Street) via the #6 Pelham Bay Park line is below ground until after Hunts Point Avenue in the southeast Bronx. The elevated route crosses the Bruckner Expressway, the Amtrak line from Penn Station to New England, the Bronx River, the Bronx River Parkway, the Cross Bronx Expressway, and the Hutchinson River Parkway. Neighborhoods are Parkchester, a late-1930s and early-1940s Metropolitan Life Insurance–sponsored housing project, and Westchester Square, with distinctive St. Peter's Church (1853–1855) and ancillary buildings and cemetery (1702-plus), seen down to the right after the Zerega Avenue station.

To get your bearings before leaving the elevated Pelham Bay Park terminal, have a look at the helpful neighborhood map. A pedestrian overpass from track level leads across the Bruckner Expressway into Pelham Bay Park. You might walk to the handsome 1925 World War Memorial rising up through the trees. Pelham Bay Park is the city's largest; paths lead north to the Bartow-Pell Mansion Museum (circa 1675, alterations 1836–1842), Orchard Beach (swimming), and City Island, a taste of New England in the Bronx.

The hike begins on the street heading northwest to the start of Burr Avenue, marked by a grassy strip to the right and small brick row houses to the left. In 2 blocks, the road angles left; at the intersection with Continental Avenue (on the left), angle slightly right to cross (left side) on a stone bridge carrying the Pelham Parkway over the Hutchinson River Parkway to another, wider bridge over the Amtrak rail line. Where the true parkway section begins at Stillwell Avenue, the first set of lights, cross over to the north-side service

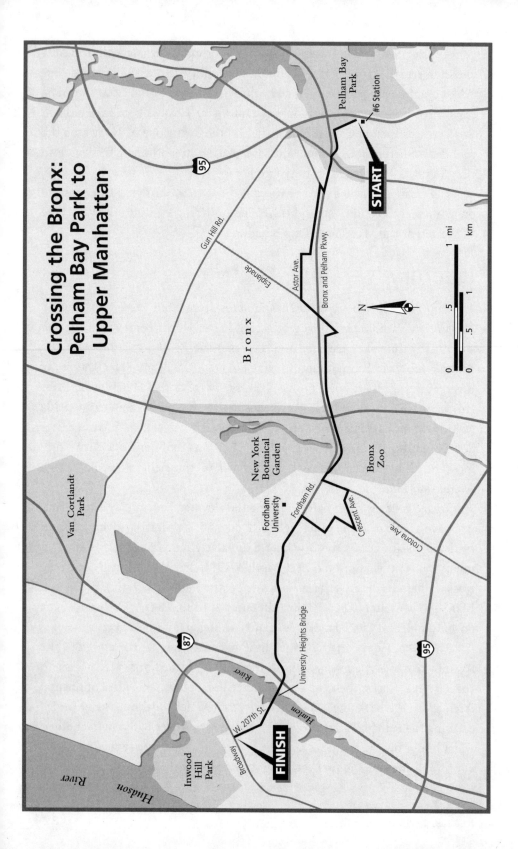

Crossing the Bronx:
Pelham Bay Park to
Upper Manhattan

95

Gun Hill Rd.

Esplanade

Astor Ave.

Bronx and Pelham Pkwy.

Bronx

Pelham Bay Park

#6 Station

START

N

0   .5   1
0   .5   1 km
1 mi

New York Botanical Garden

Bronx Zoo

Fordham University

Fordham Rd.

Crescent Ave.

Crotona Ave.

Van Cortlandt Park

87

95

University Heights Bridge

Harlem River

W. 207th St.

Broadway

FINISH

Inwood Hill Park

Hudson River

This path in the New York Botanical Garden is bordered with lush greenery.

road running in front of a continuous row of mostly single-family houses, many dating from the parkway's neighborhood development in the 1920s and 1930s. Officially known as the Bronx and Pelham Parkway, the grassy medians, leafy character, and relative tranquillity have little changed, making for a delightful walk. Pelham Gardens to the north is the kind of middle-class neighborhood that dresses up big time for Halloween and Christmas.

After a couple of blocks, turn right, walk 1 block to Astor Avenue, and turn left for attractive rows of houses on both sides. At the Esplanade and the Pelham Parkway station, the wide road angles right and left. The subway line beneath was originally built for the New York, Westchester & Boston Railway Company, which went bankrupt and was taken over by the Transit Authority in 1941 to serve the Dyre Avenue #5 train. Go left along the Esplanade to cross the intersection with Williamsbridge Road and Pelham Parkway. Four short blocks south in the attractive Morris Park neighborhood is another faintly Mediterranean-style aboveground station. Note the way the houses are sited in relation to the street pattern and their decorative brickwork.

From the Morris Park station, double back 1 block to Hone Avenue and turn left to join the south side of Pelham Parkway. Very shortly you come to the elevated White Plains Road #2 line and its enclosed 1917 station. Beneath the structure to the south and north are several blocks of restaurants, diners, fast-food outlets, and delis, providing an excellent locale to buy lunch to eat in or take to a bench along the parkway.

Continue west along the south verge, paralleling the now very busy Pelham Parkway as it intersects with the Bronx River Parkway and enters Bronx Park. The on- and off-ramps need to be carefully crossed. Once you're beyond the Bronx River Parkway crossing, the route becomes Fordham Road, passing between the Bronx Zoo (entrance to the left) and the New York Botanical Garden (right). The McDonald's on the left has rest rooms.

If you'd like to route your hike through the New York Botanical Garden, go right for 2 blocks from the north side of Pelham Parkway along the fence separating the botanical garden from Bronx Park East to the Waring Avenue Gate. Admission charges depend on how much you want to visit; the sample route here will serve as an introduction—and perhaps stimulate a longer return visit.

With signposting around you and a botanical garden map in hand, walk ahead, then go left past the Children's Garden and down to Bronx River for a path leading to Snuff Mill. This nineteenth-century building, used for parties and weddings, creates the centerpiece for a lovely wooded setting that transports you north to the Berkshires.

Continue south to the stone bridge over the Bronx River, following signs to the seasonal gardens and to the majestic forty-acre forest rising to the right. The main path leads to the flower gardens surrounding the Enid A. Haupt Conservatory, the plant shops, and the cafe, offering a good menu and outdoor seating. To continue the Fordham Road hike, leave via the Conservatory Gate to Southern Boulevard opposite Fordham University and walk south to Fordham Road.

Continuing the walk on the south side of Fordham Road, the Belmont section on the left is home to a thriving Italian immigrant community. Go left on Crotona Avenue to East 187th Street; here begins the heart of the neighborhood's restaurants, cafes, food stores, and markets celebrating Italian heritage. A Saturday visit is better than Sunday, when many shops and the market are closed. Walk west to Crescent Avenue and angle left for 3 blocks to the intersection with Arthur Avenue. Then take a hard right up Arthur Avenue for the greatest concentration of Italian restaurants, plus a few Albanian. On the right, partway up the first block, is the entrance to the lively indoor Arthur Avenue Retail Market. Stop in to pick up some osso buco, sausage, pasta, and fava beans.

At Arthur Avenue and East 187th Street, turn left; in a few blocks, the ethnic neighborhood peters out and opens onto Third Avenue. Turn right to Fordham Plaza, partly occupied by a market catering to the mostly African American community. The market fronts onto Fordham Road, the Metro-North station, and Fordham University to the right. Turn left at the Sears Building and stay on the much livelier south side of Fordham Road for the street peddlers and intense sidewalk activity. Fordham Road climbs to the Grand Concourse, a commercial intersection with the D train underground. The Concourse, lined with low-rise, mostly art-deco-style residential apart-ments, stretches left to East 138th Street and right to above East 205th Street and the Mosholu Parkway. Three more blocks westward, the Jerome Avenue el carrying the #4 train runs north to Woodlawn Cemetery and south to Yankee Stadium and Manhattan.

At West Fordham Road and University Avenue, look left and right to see the unmistakable raised rounded linear stone-faced tube carrying the old Croton Aqueduct. The path—in this section there are benches on either side—runs north into Van Cortlandt Park and Westchester County and south to High Bridge over the Harlem River. (See Escape 12 for 30 miles of aqueduct hiking paralleling the Hudson.) As Fordham Road drops down to the Harlem River, note to the right the row of attractive wooden houses on the far side of Devoe Park. The road crosses over the Major Deegan Expressway and the Metro-North Hudson Line. The shelters at either end of the University Heights Bridge (1895) center span once served a trolley line that operated until the 1950s.

The designation on the Harlem River's Manhattan side is now West 207th Street; directly ahead is the elevated #1/9 Broadway Local north to 242nd Street and Van Cortlandt Park and south to the Upper West Side, Times Square, Greenwich Village, and Lower Manhattan. If you prefer to return south staying on the surface, continue 4 blocks through a busy, largely Hispanic neighborhood to Broadway. The bus stop is left across the street. The M100 is the best route, going south to 168th Street to connect with the M5 down the West Side and the M4 to Fifth Avenue on the East Side. By staying on the M100, the route follows Amsterdam Avenue, then heads east on 125th Street. At Lexington Avenue, switch to the #4, #5, or #6 subway; the M101 or M103 down Lexington; or the M15 down Second Avenue.

For More Information

New York City Transit Authority: (718) 330–1234; www.mta.info. Subway and bus information.

Bronx Information: www.bronx.ny.us.

The Bronx County Historical Society: (718) 881–8900; www.bronxhistorical society.org.

New York Botanical Garden: (718) 817–8700; www.nybg.org.

Wildlife Conservation Society (formerly New York Zoological Society): (718) 220–5100; www.wcs.org.

6 Brooklyn Park to Park: Brooklyn Bridge to Prospect Park

This 10-mile sight-seeing hike crosses the Brooklyn Bridge and explores multiple neighborhoods, commercial districts, cultural institutions, and open spaces from Brooklyn Heights via Fort Greene Park to Prospect Park.

Itinerary at a Glance

Starting point

City Hall Park, Lower Manhattan.

Travel directions to starting point

Subway: East Side/Lexington Avenue #4, #5, or #6 to Brooklyn Bridge/City Hall and exit in front of the train; N or R to City Hall, then walk across the park to the Brooklyn Bridge footpath. West Side #2 or #3 to Park Place. Exit in front of the train and walk across Broadway and City Hall Park to the Brooklyn Bridge footpath.

Bus: From the East Side, take M103 to Park Row opposite City Hall Park; M1 down Fifth Avenue, Park Avenue South, and Broadway (weekdays only to City Hall); M15 down Second Avenue to Park Row (weekdays only), otherwise the M15 marked SOUTH FERRY to the Brooklyn Bridge underpass on Water Street. From the West Side, take M6 down Broadway to City Hall Park.

Car: Very limited parking on the street.

Return: By subway from several locations near Prospect Park, depending on where you decide to end the hike.

Difficulty level and special considerations

This mostly flat hike will be on sidewalks, except in several parks where hikers may choose grass. Any season will do, but avoid an extremely hot summer day. Fall foliage abounds on leafy streets in Cadman Plaza, Brooklyn Heights, Fort Greene, the Brooklyn

Botanic Garden, and Prospect Park. Bring water if it's a hot day; there are numerous eating places, or you can get take-out food for a picnic in a park. Get an early start, because there is much to see. The pace is slower than on strictly hiking outings. Comfort stations will be noted, and of course, you can use toilet facilities in any restaurant you patronize. One cautionary note: Avoid straying off the recommended route into densely wooded areas in Prospect Park, unless there are four or more people in your party. Otherwise the park is safe.

Introduction

Brooklyn, with its multi-ethnic population of 2.3 million, is much less visited on foot than Manhattan, yet the borough has equally intriguing neighborhoods, fine cultural institutions, and parks, and much that is of interest is surprisingly close together—ideal for this sight-seeing hike. More will be suggested than can be done in a day, and with such rich diversions, consider a second or third visit. You can stick to the straight and narrow and merely note individual destinations or, depending on your interests, include one or two side trips.

For a start, the Brooklyn Bridge has become a huge tourist attraction, and one that I never tire of, after some one hundred crossings. The pedestrian route then swings through one of the city's oldest neighborhoods, where wooden houses from the 1820s to the 1840s still stand along streets named after fruit. At the promenade in front of Brooklyn Heights, one of New York's most delightful residential districts, you will want to pause for the sweeping view of Manhattan from Midtown to the Battery then left to the harbor and Governors Island.

From the Heights, you can divert to the Middle Eastern neighborhood and antiques row on Atlantic Avenue before continuing through downtown Brooklyn along Fulton Street, with its mix of age-old business and those catering to today's inner-city population.

A big surprise awaits with the climb into Fort Greene Park. Then the route drops down into the wonderful mixture of row and freestanding housing styles from the park to Clinton Avenue. Brooklyn's richest families, some of them household names—Bristol, Otis, Pfizer, Reynolds, Sperry, Underwood —lived here until the early twentieth century. A suggested diversion includes Pratt Institute and more of Clinton Hill.

The route then follows the row-house streets in Prospect Heights up to the

The promenade at Brooklyn Heights provides a peaceful setting and a grand view
at the edge of the country's first historic district.

Grand Army Plaza, where you have the option to climb a triumphal arch, visit the vast collections in the Brooklyn Museum, stroll through the delightfully compact Brooklyn Botanic Garden, or continue the march into country-style Prospect Park. You can then return directly by subway or continue on foot through Park Slope, one of Brooklyn's most successfully reborn neighborhoods, back to Grand Army Plaza for the subway or bus along Flatbush Avenue.

Itinerary

While standing at the east side of City Hall Park, you will find you are surrounded by a substantial collection of historic buildings. Spinning clockwise, look for City Hall, New York County (Tweed) Courthouse, Surrogate's Court/Hall of Records, Municipal Building, the majestic stone towers of the Brooklyn Bridge, former Park Row newspaper headquarters, and the Woolworth Building—not bad for a quick pivot.

Cross the street carefully to reach the bridge path, and shift right for the pedestrian half (watch out for speeding bikers coming the other way). The

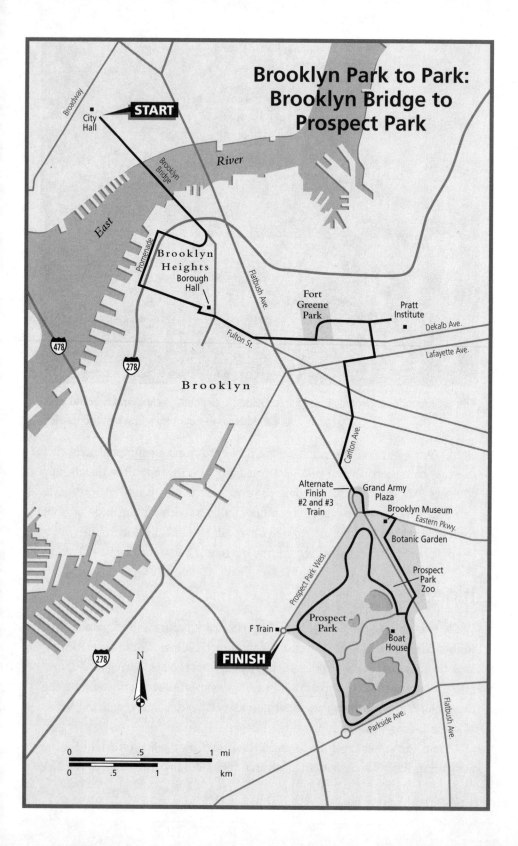

Brooklyn Park to Park: Brooklyn Bridge to Prospect Park

START

City Hall

Broadway

Brooklyn Bridge

East River

Promenade

Brooklyn Heights

Borough Hall

Flatbush Ave.

Fort Greene Park

Pratt Institute

Dekalb Ave.

Lafayette Ave.

Fulton St.

478

278

Brooklyn

Carlton Ave.

Alternate Finish #2 and #3 Train

Grand Army Plaza

Brooklyn Museum

Eastern Pkwy.

Botanic Garden

Prospect Park West

Prospect Park Zoo

Prospect Park

Boat House

F Train

FINISH

278

N

Parkside Ave.

Flatbush Ave.

0   .5   1 mi

0   .5   1 km

Prospect Park was designed to be wide open and reflect the rural nature of Brooklyn during the second half of the nineteenth century.

path rises above the traffic as it approaches the first of two towers. Where the route passes around them, the railings hold historical plaques depicting the bridge's construction, early ferryboats, and East River ship traffic. Completed in 1883, the bridge was a monumental technical achievement and made New York known around the world as the place where innovative things happened. The view is as popular now as it was then, so pause for a look south to the Upper Bay and northwest to Midtown.

Approaching the Brooklyn side, narrow steps to the left lead down to the street beneath the underpass; then turn right up to Cadman Plaza, a leafy park that runs to Borough Hall ahead and out of sight. Walking around to the right, you come to Cadman Plaza, the street. Cross and ahead take one of the fruity streets—Cranberry, Orange, or Pineapple—to the promenade, passing some early-nineteenth-century wooden houses. On Cranberry, you find the Plymouth Church of the Pilgrims, dating from 1850, and the house of Henry Ward Beecher, the antislavery clergyman. At Columbia Street, running parallel to the waterfront, you are in the midst of Jehovah's Witnesses' residences, with the *Watchtower* headquarters to the right.

The Brooklyn Heights Promenade (1950–1951) sits atop the Brooklyn-

Queens Expressway (BQE), an often congested road that is happily almost out of sight and sound. The delightful setting has all of Manhattan, the East River, and the Upper Bay out front; behind are the nineteenth-century town houses and apartments that make this neighborhood as attractive as any in the city. The Heights qualified as New York's first landmark district (1965), and lucky are those who live here and can walk to jobs in Lower Manhattan via the bridge.

Near the promenade's south end, there is a children's playground with rest rooms. Please close the gate when you enter and leave. From the end of the promenade, you can see how the elevated BQE slices right through the industrial and residential neighborhoods to the south. If you want something to eat, Montague Street, starting at the playground, is a most attractive commercial strip; a block here is reminiscent of Boston's Boylston Street, with iron steps leading up and down to two levels of storefronts.

Otherwise, take Remsen, which aims straight at Brooklyn's Borough Hall, the former city hall dating from 1846–1851 before the 1898 amalgamation. On the way, you pass Romanesque Our Lady of Lebanon (Maronite) Roman Catholic Church (1844–1845) at Henry Street. The bronze doors facing south and west depict Norman castles and churches and a three-funneled ocean liner—the *Ile de France*. They were salvaged from the French liner *Normandie,* which burned in February 1942 at Pier 88 during conversion into a troopship.

For a diversion, take Henry or Clinton right 3 blocks to Atlantic Avenue for a several-block section of Middle Eastern restaurants, specialty shops, and antiques stores.

Continue along Remsen to Borough Hall, a Greek Revival–style building (1846–1851) located at the south end of Cadman Plaza. Walk around the columned frontage, then head across the busy street to the Fulton Street Mall. Narrowed for wider sidewalks and with traffic limited to buses and taxis, the street is overwhelmingly geared to an African American clientele and is as lively as any commercial strip you will find in Brooklyn.

Historic holdovers include Gage & Tollner (right side at 372 Fulton Street), a restaurant established in 1879 and worth a look inside, even if you're not stopping for a meal, for its gaslight chandeliers, arched mirrors, Victorian dining car atmosphere, and the staff, some of whom have been here for years. Also on the right the former Abraham & Straus (buildings 1885, 1929, 1935) is now a Macy's and the mall's anchor store. The 1906–1908 former Dime Savings Bank Building, now Washington Mutual (left), is a must-see inside—a monumental interior that would have impressed and even overwhelmed immigrants who came to start a savings account. Note the number of live tellers compared to the relatively few automatic teller machines. One block more (angle left onto DeKalb to the corner with Flatbush Avenue Extension) is Junior's, a landmark deli and take-out restaurant (since 1929) that draws every race and religion to its dining room, counter, and takeout. Longtime patrons know about Junior's cheesecake. Plain is always best.

Follow DeKalb Avenue past L.I. University and a hospital to Fort Greene Park, rising steeply to a high mound atop which is a 148-foot Doric column with a bronze brazier. The 1908-built monument, known as the Prison Ships Martyrs' Monument, is dedicated to more than 11,500 Revolutionary War sailors and soldiers who were imprisoned and later died on decommissioned British ships in Wallabout Bay, the location of the Brooklyn Navy Yard (seen below through the trees). Stanford White, the architect, was also responsible for the elaborate but closed Doric-temple-style comfort station.

Walk down the hill to the outstanding row of brownstone residences facing the park, built in the 1860s and beautifully maintained. By taking Willoughby Street, you are entering the Fort Greene and Clinton Hill Historic District (some blocks only). It's a mixed neighborhood, racially and architecturally, from clapboard houses to low-rise projects. Turn right onto Clinton Avenue—unless you would like to continue a few more blocks to Pratt Institute. Established by Charles Pratt in 1887, a partner with John D. Rockefeller, Pratt is known for arts and design, architecture, liberal arts, and information and library science; the campus is architecturally significant.

Along Clinton are some distinguished mansions. No. 232 was the Charles Pratt Italianate-style house (1875), now St. Joseph's College; No. 229 was built in 1895 in Georgian/Renaissance Revival style for a Pratt son, and is now a foreign students' residence; No. 241 is an 1890 Richardson Romanesque built for another son and now the Roman Catholic Bishop of Brooklyn's residence; and No. 245, a Georgian Revival from 1901, was for a third son and part of St. Joseph's. Along on the right at No. 284 is an 1854 Newport stick-and-shingle-style house.

At Lafayette, turn right, then in 4 blocks turn left onto Carlton Avenue, cross industrial Atlantic Avenue and the Long Island Rail Road cut to Flatbush Avenue, and angle left up to Parisian-style Grand Army Plaza, with the same swirling traffic. Pass the Montauk Club, a Venetian Gothic palazzo (1891) on the right, and arrive at the traffic circle anchored by the Soldiers' and Sailors' Memorial Arch (1892). The roof is open on summer Saturdays for the view back to downtown Brooklyn, distant Manhattan, Prospect Park, and the endlessly fascinating urban sprawl of Bedford-Stuyvesant and Crown Heights. The plainish hulk of the Brooklyn Public Library faces the plaza; to the left, Eastern Parkway, the world's first six-lane parkway, begins. (It was designed by Olmsted and Vaux.)

One long block leads to the entrance of the Brooklyn Botanic Garden, a fifty-two-acre gem of little parks within the larger park. It is noted for its wisteria garden, rose garden, cherry orchard, Shakespeare Garden, scented garden for the blind, outstanding Japanese hill and pond garden (popular for wedding photos), children's garden program, and several greenhouses (rest rooms nearby). The garden has popular seasonal plant sales. If you're heading to Prospect Park, you can exit beyond the children's garden then cross Flatbush Avenue. Returning through the garden via a loop to the way in, go right to the Brooklyn Museum of Art—where you could easily spend the day looking at the Egyptian collection, Asian and African art, and twenty-one period rooms depicting residential life in New York City.

Back at the Grand Army Plaza, take the path to the left of Prospect Park's road entrance that leads down into a hollow and through a bridge tunnel known as the Endale Arch (1867). As you exit the tunnel, there is a long-range meadow view framed by woods with no sign of the city in sight. Frederick Law Olmsted and Charles Vaux, of Central Park and Fort Greene Park fame, wanted to create a rural setting that was reflective of what had been here before the surrounding neighborhoods began to develop.

There are a number of sights to visit, or you can just walk the length of the dogleg Long Meadow to the far side at Prospect Park Southwest and turn right onto 15th Street for the F train back to Manhattan. The street and park path angles can easily confuse, and you may end up where you don't want to be. I know from personal experiences—plural!

But to explore further, follow the drive to the left and you will come to the Wildlife Center, a small zoo designed for children (rest rooms here), a grand carousel, and the white-shingled Lefferts Homestead (1783), representative of a Dutch-style farmhouse, which now is a children's program center. The drive continues past the Boathouse, a handsome white terra-cotta 1904 classical-style building with terraced steps leading down to water. The inside, used variously as a parks department interpretive center and for catered parties, features a vaulted ceiling decorated with Guastavino green tiles—similar in style to the Oyster Bar at Grand Central Terminal and Guastavino, the vaulted restaurant tucked in under the Queensboro Bridge approach near First Avenue. The drive and paths loop along either side of Prospect Lake. Just outside the park near the carousel is the Prospect Park station for the Q train back to Manhattan. Another stop for the Q is Parkside at the park's southeast corner.

Returning to Endale Gate, instead of taking the drive to the left, take the path to the right. You'll pass the Italianate Litchfield House (1854–1857), now used by the parks department; the redbrick Picnic House and 1910 Palladian Tennis House (for weddings and catered affairs) to the left; and then enclosed Quaker Hill Friends Cemetery, which predated the park. Permission, or a tour, is needed to enter. Leaving the park onto Prospect Park West, the perpendicular streets and right angled avenues—Eighth, Seventh, and Sixth—are worth a wander to see some of the finest row-house residential architecture in New York, plus the occasional leftover mansions-turned-schools. Known as Park Slope, the neighborhood, much of it designated a historic district, is hugely popular to live in. It slopes down literally—and also in rent levels—to the Gowanus Canal and then up into Carroll Gardens. By following Park Slope West back to Grand Army Plaza, you'll find the station entrance for the #2 and #3 trains to Manhattan located on the plaza's far side toward downtown Brooklyn. For the East Side, change at Nevins Street (cross the platform) to the #4 (#5 weekdays only).

For More Information

New York City Transit Authority: (718) 330–1234; www.mta.info. Subway and bus information.

Brooklyn Botanic Garden: (718) 623–7200; www.bbg.org.

Brooklyn Information & Culture: www.brooklynX.org or www.brooklynonline.com.

Brooklyn Museum: (718) 638–5000; www.brooklynart.org/.

Lefferts Homestead: (718) 789–2822.

Prospect Park: (718) 965–8999; www.prospectpark.org.

Prospect Park Wildlife Center: (718) 399–7339.

Gage & Tollner: 372 Fulton Street; (718) 875–5181; www.gageandtollner.com.

Junior's Restaurant: 386 Flatbush Avenue Extension; (718) 852–5257.

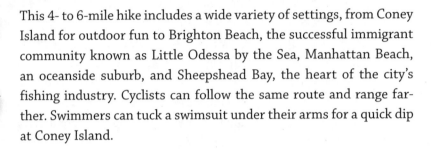

By the Seaside: Coney Island, Brighton Beach, and Sheepshead Bay

ESCAPE **7**

This 4- to 6-mile hike includes a wide variety of settings, from Coney Island for outdoor fun to Brighton Beach, the successful immigrant community known as Little Odessa by the Sea, Manhattan Beach, an oceanside suburb, and Sheepshead Bay, the heart of the city's fishing industry. Cyclists can follow the same route and range farther. Swimmers can tuck a swimsuit under their arms for a quick dip at Coney Island.

Itinerary at a Glance

Starting point

Coney Island, Stillwell Avenue subway station.

Travel directions to starting point

Subway: There are a variety of trains to Coney Island, but the F train (elevated in Brooklyn) from Manhattan is recommended for the outbound trip because of the views. The W (partly elevated in Brooklyn) also operates from Manhattan.

Car: East River bridges or Brooklyn Battery Tunnel then Brooklyn-Queens Expressway, Gowanus Expressway, and Shore Parkway to the Coney Island exit; park close to the boardwalk.

Return: The Q train either Manhattan-bound or, for drivers to return to their cars, Coney Island–bound (Stillwell Avenue).

Bicycle: There are a variety of routes to and from Coney Island, Brighton Beach, and Sheepshead Bay. From the Brooklyn Bridge, go to relatively quiet Henry Street in Brooklyn Heights, then continue across Atlantic into Cobble Hill and Carroll Gardens as far as Union Street. Turn left onto Union, crossing the Gowanus Canal to Third Avenue, then go right and left on 3rd Street up to Prospect Park. Use the park drive to Prospect Park South and exit via Fort

Hamilton Parkway 3 blocks to Ocean Parkway. The world's first dedicated cycling path runs for 5 straight miles along Ocean Parkway to the Coney Island Boardwalk. While bicycles are permitted only from 5:00 to 10:00 A.M., you can walk your bike or use parallel Surf Avenue west toward Sea Gate or right to Brighton Beach. From Sheepshead Bay, Bedford Avenue has a 7-mile-long on-street bike lane to Eastern Parkway and Bergen Street, then left to downtown Brooklyn. For dedicated on-street bike lanes and a short greenway, use Eastern Parkway to Prospect Park, exit the park onto 2nd Street down to Fourth Avenue, then turn left onto 3rd Street and go right across the Gowanus Canal to Clinton Street in Carroll Gardens. Go right onto Clinton through Cobble Hill, across Atlantic Avenue to Brooklyn Heights, and back across the Brooklyn Bridge.

Difficulty level and special considerations

The entire walk is flat (it's also mostly flat if you're cycling out and back), and the surfaces vary among pavement, wooden boardwalks, and even sand. The busiest period is a summer weekend, and the best time to enjoy the seaside without the crowds is an off-season Saturday or Sunday— even in the dead of winter on a bright sunny day. The bustling commercial activity goes on under the el at Brighton Beach regardless of the month. Bring water, sunscreen, and a hat. There are lots of interesting places to eat or, better still, buy lunch locally and take it to the beach or boardwalk. Once you're at the boardwalk, the walking part could take as little as two hours, but if you stop to sight-see and make several diversions, the outing can easily last until midafternoon.

Introduction

Few city walks can combine such contrasts in the space of one short day, with the varied ingredients of the beach and boardwalk, strongly ethnic neighborhoods, leafy residential streets, fishing docks, an amusement park, the aquarium, and even a highly popular new minor-league baseball stadium.

Coney Island's has-been reputation is now changing for the positive with the construction of a new baseball park on the site of old Steeplechase Park. The ripple effect and some new middle-class housing have turned the place around, but the boardwalk and the beach give the same invigorating lift as always.

The 2.5-mile boardwalk, running between Sea Gate and Manhattan

Beach, is a wide pedestrian boulevard where you can enjoy watching local residents chatting and playing games in their front yards or have a meal at one of Brighton Beach's outdoor cafes. Cyclists are welcome on the boardwalk until 10:00 A.M.

Nestled under the elevated subway line is a major commercial strip of restaurants, many Russian or Ukrainian, fish markets, delicatessens, and food and clothing peddlers. The shadows of the el and the rattle of the trains create a true old-time New York atmosphere that no longer exists in Manhattan, but sure does in parts of Brooklyn, the Bronx, and Queens.

The walking pace quickens as you leave Brighton Beach for Manhattan Beach, where the residential architecture varies from 1920s mock Tudor to 1950s brick and some recent large trophy houses built on small plots of land. The route then crosses a footbridge to Sheepshead Bay, where party fishing boats leave once or twice a day for deep-sea and bottom fishing. The best time for a visit is after 3:00 P.M., when the boats begin to return and the catch that is not taken home gets sold for bargain prices right on the docks.

Itinerary

The F train ride will be the start for those using public transit. Once you're beyond downtown Brooklyn, the line rises high over the Gowanus Canal, an industrial waterway that has gone all quiet. But the best views are of the Brooklyn and Manhattan skylines before the train dives into a tunnel to then rise at Ditmas Avenue over the old BMT Culver Line trestle. From the train window, you get a semi-aerial view of Borough Park, Bensonhurst, and the two towers of the Verrazano-Narrows Bridge.

The line slides onto Coney Island at the vast Stillwell Avenue station, the end of the line for several subway routes. The station is under reconstruction so expect service alterations. At one time, when Coney Island was the best-known day resort in the world, a million visitors would arrive on a hot summer Saturday or Sunday. Ahead to the left and right were Steeplechase Park (1897), Luna Park (1903), and Dreamland (1904), but the last of the three, Steeplechase, closed in 1964. Only the 1,000-foot pier remains, and it's worth walking out to the end to watch the fisherfolk trying their luck for blues, fluke, flounder, and stripers.

Walking ahead, to the left of Nathan's Famous (since 1916) for hot dogs, Astroland hangs on and offers midway-type attractions, amusement park rides,

The 2.5-mile-long Boardwalk at Brighton Beach parallels a wide sandy beach.

and three notable structures, the Wonder Wheel (Ferris wheel, 1918–1920), Cyclone (roller coaster, 1927), and stylish B&B Carousel. The structure rising to the right is the Parachute Jump, built for the 1939–1940 World's Fair and later moved here. It's officially stabilized, so no longer can you feel the sensation of free fall. New to the neighborhood, west of West 17th Street between Surf Avenue and the boardwalk, is KeySpan Park, home of the Brooklyn Cyclones, a New York Mets farm team. Ticket information is below.

The boardwalk, running from the entrance of Sea Gate, a private community to the right, facing the ocean, to the edge of Manhattan Beach, was first constructed in 1923 to alleviate congestion for the crowds—visitors and then residents—who flocked here. It's up to 40 feet wide and almost 3 miles long, and consists of some 1.3 million boards and more than fifteen million screws and nails. Maintenance is mighty expensive.

It is a delight to be out in the open with views to Staten Island, North Jersey's Atlantic Highlands, the tip of the Rockaway Peninsula at Breezy Point, and the mostly brick low-rise and high-rise apartments to the left of the boardwalk and inland. The New York Aquarium moved here in 1957 and offers children the

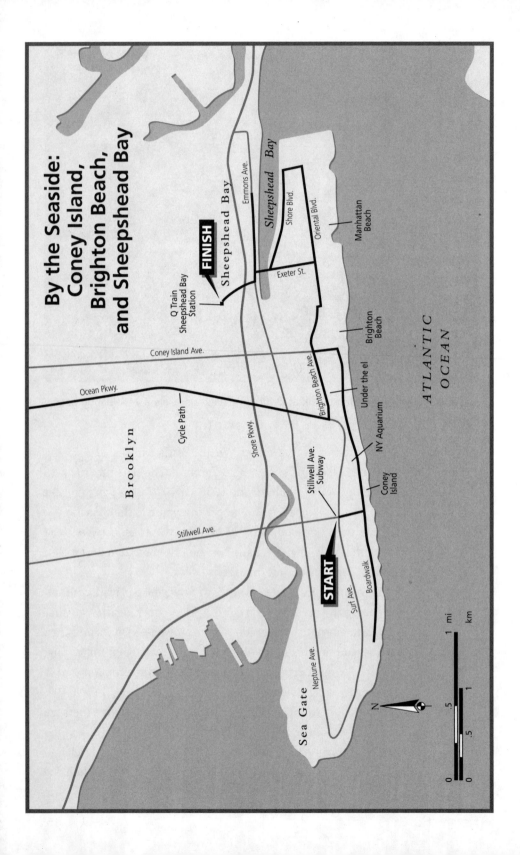

By the Seaside:
Coney Island, Brighton Beach, and Sheepshead Bay

Brooklyn

Sea Gate

Coney Island Ave.

Ocean Pkwy.

Cycle Path

Shore Pkwy.

Stillwell Ave.

Stillwell Ave. Subway

Neptune Ave.

Surf Ave.

Boardwalk

START

NY Aquarium

Coney Island

Under the el

Brighton Beach Ave.

Brighton Beach

ATLANTIC OCEAN

Manhattan Beach

Oriental Blvd.

Shore Blvd.

Emmons Ave.

Exeter St.

Sheepshead Bay

Sheepshead Bay

Q Train Sheepshead Bay Station

FINISH

N

1 mi

km

0   .5   1

0   .5   1

excitement of seeing whales, dolphins, penguins, octopi, and electric eels.

Once a major hotel resort, Brighton Beach today is a thriving community made up largely of recent Russians and Ukrainian immigrants, many from Odessa—hence its nickname as Little Odessa by the Sea. Residents will be out in force on a sunny day, wearing heavy coats and furs in winter, the season I most enjoy coming here. Often the men play chess and dominoes together while the women chat in a circle of chairs brought from nearby apartments. In winter, the broad beach will see a few strollers, some with metal detectors, and frolicking dogs.

Boardwalk outdoor cafes beckon for a meal or within when it's cold, for seafood, shellfish, and Russian favorites, many of which you will also find under the el, two blocks inland. Turn left at the new apartments, Oceana and Seacoast, on the site of the old Brighton Beach Bath and Racquet Club, and walk to the corner where the el makes a sharp turn and shelters Brighton Beach Avenue (running beneath to the left). Here in the shadows, you will find an old-fashioned only-in-New-York scene of street sellers, kiosks, and mostly small stores catering to the Russian and Ukrainian community. If it's lunchtime, there are lots of places to eat, with cheap lunch menus, or take-out food such as blinis (pancakes) with sour cream, blintzes (thin pancakes), knishes (fried or baked turnovers) filled with meat or potatoes, kasha (buckwheat or other grain), stuffed eggplant, and much more.

Down on the right, walk into M&I International for an amazingly efficient delicatessen ruled over by uniformed women selling all manner of spiced meats and sausages, salted fish, herring, cheeses, breads, cold cuts, prepared salads, canned goods from Mother Russia or Ukraine, and much more. Take your time absorbing the atmosphere as well as some of the unfamiliar foods. At Ocean Parkway (the end of the long bicycle path from Prospect Park), cross the street and walk back under the el; when it turns left, stay on Brighton Beach Avenue, now without its cover. Some more attractive stores line the left-hand side. Beyond the new mid- and high-rise blocks, there are several wonderfully fanciful art deco low-rise apartment houses. Look at the sunburst decoration in the recessed entrances and the purely decorative structures up on the roof.

Brighton Beach Avenue ends at the Manhattan Beach line, and another world opens up when you walk first right, then left onto Oriental Avenue. A major hotel district at the turn of the twentieth century, Manhattan Beach is now a sharply defined suburb of houses dating from the 1920s to today, most of the newest much larger and replacing smaller dwellings. The cross streets have English names starting with A (Amherst) and ending at P (Pembroke) at the entrance to Kingsborough Community College, part of City University.

For a faster walk after all the dawdling of the last few hours, take any of the first few streets to the right down to the esplanade and go left along the seafront. Otherwise, walk straight ahead to the community college gates and go left 1 long block to Sheepshead Bay. Follow Shore Boulevard back along a promenade across from the fishing fleet piers as far as the wooden footbridge, and take it to the other side. If you do not wish to make this 25-block loop, then turn left off Oriental onto Exeter Street, which in 2 long leafy blocks runs into the footbridge.

The bridge once linked a racecourse on the north side with the horse paddock on the site of present Manhattan Beach. On the far side, the long, low Mediterranean-style building once housed the 2,800-seat Lundy Bros. Restaurant, which opened in 1934 and closed in 1979. It's been open again since 1995 on a smaller scale, with 800 seats. Emmons Avenue was seafood restaurant row, and there still are about a dozen places of varying quality.

The big show along Emmons is at the piers to the right, where several generations of boat owners operate fishing cruises aboard more than a dozen party boats from the simple to the plush—with heated handrails and TVs. Catering to different clienteles, the serious boats leave the earliest; most are usually back by 3:00 or 4:00 P.M. Popular fish include blackfish, bluefish, fluke, flounder, ling, and sea bass. The boats may announce their arrival with a horn, and local residents come down to buy the leftover catch at cheap prices. Roman numerals II through VII are often added to the boats' names— *Amberjack, Apache, Blue Sea, Brooklyn, Dorothy B,* and *Zephyr B*—to indicate how many of these same names came before. The daily scene has gone on for decades; long may it continue.

To return to the subway, walk back along Emmons to Sheepshead Bay Road, turning right at the big Greek diner, and follow the road under Shore Parkway to an attractive small-store commercial strip that angles left toward the subway overpass. Film buffs may recognize the setting for the Al Pacino, Alec Baldwin, Jack Lemmon film *Glengarry Glen Ross*. At the underpass, the Q train entrance is to the left and up one flight for trains back to Manhattan or back to Coney Island on a seaside trestle above Brighton Beach Avenue. Cyclists can use Bedford Avenue, which starts at the piers and heads inland for 6 miles to Eastern Parkway.

The *Zephyr V* is one of a dozen party fishing boats that make daily trips from the row of piers at Sheepshead Bay.

For More Information

New York City Transit Authority: (718) 330–1234; www.mta.info. Subway and bus information.

Brooklyn Information & Culture: www.brooklynX.org or www.brooklynonline.com.

Brooklyn Cyclones: (718) 449–8497; www.brooklyncyclones.com. Professional baseball team, Coney Island.

Brighton Beach: (718) 891–0800; www.brightonbeach.com.

Coney Island: www.coneyisland.org.

Astroland: (718) 265–2100; www.astroland.com.

New York Aquarium: (718) 265–FISH; www.nyaquarium.com.

Dorothy B VIII: Pier 6, Emmons Avenue; (718) 646–4057; www.dorothyb.com. Sheepshead Bay fishing boat.

Lundy Bros. Restaurant: 1901 Emmons Avenue; (718) 743–0022 www.lundybros.com.

ESCAPE 8

Brooklyn: Sunset Park to Bay Ridge

This urban and shoreline walk and cycle route of about 6 to 7 miles begins in Sunset Park, a lively Brooklyn Chinese and Hispanic neighborhood; passes up through Owls Head Park overlooking New York Harbor; then drops down to the Shore Parkway path and skirts Bay Ridge to Fort Hamilton, Dyker Beach, and Bath Beach. Cyclists will find the route of considerable interest and may wish to extend it beyond Bay Ridge to Coney Island.

Itinerary at a Glance

Starting point

Sunset Park, Brooklyn—36th Street and Fourth Avenue subway station.

Travel directions to starting point

Subway: The N, R, M, and W trains from Manhattan all serve Sunset Park.

Bus: For an alternative surface route in Brooklyn, take any number of subway routes from Manhattan to either Atlantic Avenue or Pacific Street in downtown Brooklyn, and on Flatbush Avenue, take the B63 along Fifth Avenue to 36th Street, Sunset Park.

Car: Take the Brooklyn-Battery Tunnel and the Gowanus Expressway to 39th Street and Third Avenue, Sunset Park, and use the Greenwood Cemetery Garage between Fourth and Fifth Avenues and 34th and 35th Streets.

Bicycle: From the Brooklyn Bridge, take Henry Street in Brooklyn Heights across Atlantic Avenue into Cobble Hill and Carroll Gardens, then turn left onto Union Street, cross the Gowanus Canal, and turn right onto Fifth, which runs into Sunset Park past Greenwood Cemetery.

Difficulty level and special considerations

Regardless of how far beyond Bay Ridge you go, the hike has gentle slopes in Sunset Park and in Owls Head Park. Most of the route is on sidewalks or paved paths. Cyclists use the street along the same route; the Shore Parkway path accommodates both cyclists and hikers. There are oodles of multi-ethnic places to buy food—especially Asian and Latino outlets in Sunset Park—and put together a picnic for Owls Head Park, with its terrific view of the harbor. Public rest room facilities are scarce, so you may need to patronize a restaurant. In summer, Sunset Park will be urban hot, but if you get an early start, you can be by the water by noon.

Introduction

Brooklyn is the best of the five boroughs for urban hiking, because it's so easy to combine the great out-of-doors along the shoreline with the lively neighborhoods that make New York so fascinatingly multifaceted.

In this case, the first neighborhood is Sunset Park, a community once tied to an active shipping industry at its doorstep. When containerization took the business to New Jersey and the elevated Gowanus Expressway split it in half, the area fell on hard times. In recent years, mainly Chinese immigrants have poured into the section straddling Eighth Avenue, and Puerto Ricans, Dominicans, and Mexicans have settled along Fifth Avenue, creating two contrasting commercial strips to visit and to sample the food.

The adjoining community of Bay Ridge is altogether different, settled mostly by European immigrants from Scandinavia and Italy, once a rich suburb of large houses but, since the coming of the subway in 1915, more middle class and semiurban. While suggested diversions will nudge you inland to explore a few residential blocks, the bulk of the route is along the shoreline, beginning at a virtually unknown gem of a park that overlooks the Upper New York Bay opposite Staten Island.

The waterside path, removed from most of the traffic noise, passes beneath the Verrazano-Narrows Bridge and skirts Fort Hamilton to parallel Gravesend Bay. From here, there is a choice: You can loop back through Bay Ridge to explore its parks and commercial heart, or continue alongside the Shore Parkway for the final stretch past Dyker Beach to Bensonhurst, just short of Coney Island. All options have convenient access to subway lines and to recommended bike routes.

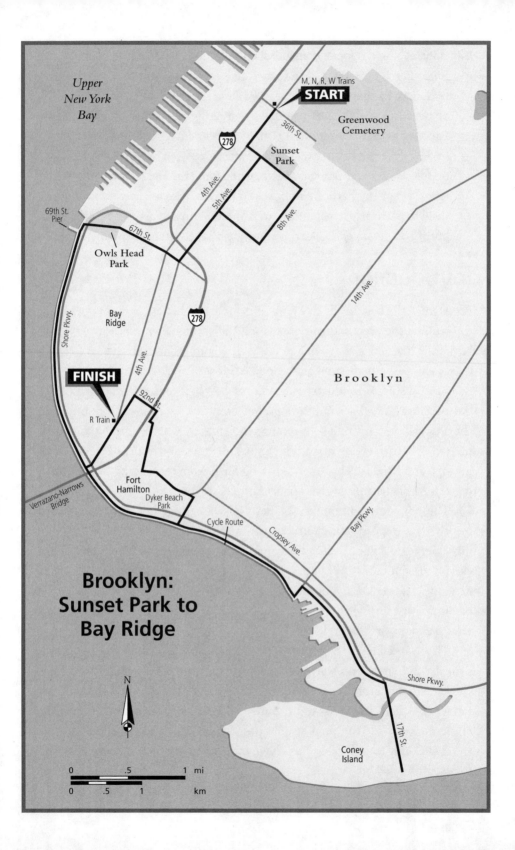

**Brooklyn:
Sunset Park to
Bay Ridge**

Upper
New York
Bay

M, N, R, W Trains
START

Greenwood
Cemetery

278

36th St.

Sunset
Park

4th Ave.

5th Ave.

8th Ave.

69th St.
Pier

67th St.

Owls Head
Park

Shore Pkwy.

Bay
Ridge

278

14th Ave.

Brooklyn

4th Ave.

FINISH

92nd St.

R Train

Verrazano-Narrows
Bridge

Fort
Hamilton

Dyker Beach
Park

Cycle Route

Cropsey Ave.

Bay Pkwy.

Shore Pkwy.

17th St.

N

Coney
Island

0   .5   1 mi

0   .5   1   km

Itinerary

Starting out at 36th Street and Fourth Avenue, the latter a fairly dull broad boulevard, walk ahead to St. Michael's Roman Catholic Church with its tapered beehive spire that somewhat resembles Sacre Coeur in Paris. Built in 1905, it is by far the tallest structure around. The side streets sloping down to the elevated expressway and upward to Fifth Avenue and beyond show off some splendid bow-fronted row houses with elaborate cornices, and many adjacent blocks are on the National Register of Historic Places. Walk up 43rd Street for a repetitive block of brownstones built about 1885.

Fifth Avenue is much livelier, and between 41st and 43rd Streets, it skirts the Sunset Park that lent its name to the neighborhood in the late 1960s. Formerly, the northern section was called Gowanus and the southern Bay Ridge; the latter now starts on the far side of the elevated freeway ahead. Fifth Avenue is Latino, mostly Puerto Rican, Dominican, and Mexican; farther up the slope, the parallel Eighth Avenue is Asian, mostly Chinese. It's well worth making a loop up and back to take in thriving but ethnically very different commercial centers.

The Chinese community got going when recent immigrants found Chinatown and Flushing too expensive. Some Chinese work locally in garment factories, and others commute via the direct subway lines to Chinatown.

Fifth Avenue quiets down as it approaches Bay Ridge, passing beneath the Gowanus Expressway and above the Bay Ridge Rail Line that connects the car-float freight car facilities on the waterfront with the Long Island Rail Road. Many of New York City's subway cars arrive at these docks, where small diesel engines shunt them onto the transit system.

At 67th Street, turn right and walk downhill to Owl Heads Park, a grassy mound that rises up ahead. Once you're atop the knoll, the Owls Head Sanitation Plant and Transfer Station is down to the right. You look well over it to the distant Manhattan skyline, Governors Island, Bayonne, New Jersey, and Staten Island. The park is clean and reasonably well tended, and the slope down to the shore is an ideal spot for a picnic on grass or a bench if the ground is damp.

At the bottom of the park, cross Shore Road and take the path that passes under Shore Parkway. Ahead is a broad recreation pier jutting out into the Upper Bay. Residents will be fishing, reading, and enjoying the open air; in the Upper Bay, ships will be at anchor and heading to Port Newark and

Elizabethport. In the late afternoon from May into October, cruise ships file out through the Narrows to the Caribbean, Bermuda, Canada, and England. Before the present pier was constructed, 69th Street, Bay Ridge, led to a ferry slip that served St. George on Staten Island, a service that was eliminated when the Verrazano-Narrows Bridge opened in November 1964.

The shore walk swings gently around the perimeter of Bay Ridge, revealing up to the left an eclectic mixture of freestanding and attached houses, low-rise apartments, and the Georgian-style Fort Hamilton High School. Pedestrian ramps occasionally connect the path to Shore Road, making a worthwhile diversion into the residential neighborhood then back to the harbor path.

The view from under the Verrazano-Narrows Bridge is across to Fort Wadsworth on the Staten Island side then left along Midland and South Beaches to Raritan Bay and New Jersey's Atlantic Highlands. A Staten Island hike and cycle route follows the Staten shoreline opposite (see Escape 11). There is no pedestrian or bike path across the bridge, however; access is via the Staten Island Ferry. Bus riders may cross the bridge using the S53 and S79 along Fourth Avenue, Bay Ridge, between 92nd and 86th Streets. The Narrows between Bay Ridge and Staten Island is well named, and the tides often result in choppy waters close to shore. The setting with the sweeping suspension bridge overheard is particularly lovely at sunset.

A ramp just before the bridge span leads over Shore Parkway and into a leafy park at the end of Fourth Avenue, the main street for Bay Ridge. It was once called Yellow Hook because of the yellow clay, but a yellow fever epidemic in 1848–1849 gave the name a bad connotation, so the community became Bay Ridge. Six blocks along Fourth Avenue lead to the R train terminal at 95th Street.

If you're game for a longer outing, follow the shore path around to the left; you are now looking across Gravesend Bay to Coney Island. Fort Hamilton, a still-active military complex and recruiting station, rises to the left. It includes 1825–1831 fortifications, part of the harbor defenses that also encompass Fort Wadsworth next to the Verrazano-Narrows Bridge on Staten Island, Castle Clinton at the Battery in Manhattan, and Castle Williams on Governors Island. For a short loop, turn inland at Dyker Beach Park, pass in front of the Fort Hamilton Veterans' Hospital on 92nd Street, and stay left along the government compound past neo-Georgian-style Poly Prep Country Day School (1924). Use the 92nd Street overpass above the Gowanus Expressway to Fifth Avenue and turn left for the R train station. Cyclists may follow this same route or continue along the shoreside bike-pedestrian path, which then shifts to a local street that leads to Coney Island Creek and the Cropsey Avenue Bridge onto Coney Island. After crossing Neptune and Mermaid Avenues, turn left onto Surf, and it's but a mile to Ocean Parkway's separate bike path north to Prospect Park and downtown Brooklyn.

For More Information

New York City Transit Authority: (718) 330–1234; www.mta.info. Subway and bus information.

Brooklyn Information & Culture: www.brooklynX.org.

Jamaica Bay Wildlife Refuge

This outing combines perhaps 5 miles of hiking and walking to and through a wildlife reserve located within the city boundaries, where both casual and serious nature lovers and bird-watchers come together to hunt their gentle prey with binoculars and cameras.

Itinerary at a Glance

Starting point

Entrance to Jamaica Bay Wildlife Refuge, Queens.

Travel directions to starting point

Subway: Take the A train from Manhattan marked FAR ROCKAWAY (*not* LEFFERTS BOULEVARD) to the Broad Channel station, one stop past Howard Beach and one stop short of the Rockaway Peninsula. Walk west from the station through the community of Broad Channel to Cross Bay Boulevard, cross over to the far side, and turn right. Continue beyond the edge of town; the path to the refuge entrance is on the left about twenty minutes after leaving the station.

Bus: First take the A train marked either LEFFERTS BOULEVARD or FAR ROCKAWAY to Rockaway Boulevard station and transfer to the Q21 (Green Bus Lines) or the Q53 (Triboro Coach) directly to Jamaica Bay Wildlife. The Q53 originates at the Woodside/61st Street station of the #7 Flushing line and travels south, crossing the E, F, G, V, R, J, and A lines. The subway-bus route is only for those who do not want to walk the twenty minutes from the subway station and back and who do not mind waiting for, in this case, infrequent buses.

Car: Take the Belt Parkway eastward to exit 17S, Cross Bay Boulevard, and go south to the refuge on the right. Free parking.

Difficulty level and special considerations

The outing is a gentle one that can be enjoyed at any time of the year. While summer is the most popular, the refuge is at its most crowded, and a hot day can be especially hot out in the marshes. Spring, fall, and winter are better times, perhaps depending on what kind of wildlife you are seeking. If seeing a particular species doesn't matter, then just go, because there is always plenty to spot. Take binoculars, water, and bug juice in summer. Check for ticks and mosquitoes in season, and ask the park rangers about their presence. If you're planning to make a day of it, take food; there isn't much to choose from in Broad Channel. Picnic tables but no shelter are available, and if it starts to rain, take shelter inside the park headquarters. You might wish to call ahead to learn if there is a special program that is worth attending.

Introduction

Jamaica Bay Wildlife Refuge is a 9,155-acre unit of Gateway National Recreation Area, and is unique in being a federal facility within a city. For urban dwellers, it's as close as you can get to nature without venturing to real country upstate, and it's available for the price of a subway or bus fare.

The expansive refuge, within sight of the Manhattan skyline and often beneath the flight patterns at JFK Airport, is surprisingly a largely artificial creation. In the early 1950s, in order to build up the Transit Authority's railway embankment, to protect it from flooding from Jamaica Bay, sand was dredged from two sections of the bay. The depressions and some dike building became the East and West Ponds, and birds migrating along the Atlantic Flyway were immediately attracted to the fresh water for feeding, nesting, and resting. Other species soon became permanent residents.

Early fall sees migrating shorebirds, flycatchers, and warblers. In late fall, look for waterfowl, hawks, and finches; in winter, horned grebes, mute swans, grackles, sparrows, starlings, ducks, geese, and gulls. Spring witnesses reverse migration, and summer is breeding season.

The visitor center has flyers listing birds by season and sighting frequency, plus guides to the animals, plants, trees, and fish. Some are free and some command a very modest price. The facility is free and is open all year except for Christmas and New Year's Day.

Itinerary

If you're coming by subway, as most will, the A train surfaces on the Brooklyn/Queens boundary at Grant Avenue. After Rockaway Boulevard, the line swings right onto a former Long Island Rail Road right-of-way. Following stops at Aqueduct Racetrack and Howard Beach (for connecting buses to JFK), the train begins to climb a causeway, and looking out the window, you have the sensation of putting out to sea. The open water and tidal marshes stretch almost as far as the eye can see. The line skirts the long, slim East Pond and slows to stop at the Broad Channel station.

Walk west through a single-family-house community that started as a fishing and oystering camp, then graduated to a summer community and finally a permanent town of about 2,700 inhabitants who now own the land they used to rent. Broad Channel itself has few services, and the residents like it that way, giving visitors, whether on foot or in a car, little reason to pause.

At busy Cross Bay Boulevard, cross to the far side, turn right, and continue for about ten minutes into a brushy area where a path will angle left to the Jamaica Bay Wildlife Refuge visitor center. Here, you will be welcomed by park rangers who sign you in, hand out and sell literature, and answer questions. The center has exhibits, an illustrated presentation, an occasional lecture, and is the starting point for guided walks.

Most people pick up the *Trail Guide to the West Pond* (charge) and the *Birds of the Jamaica Bay Wildlife Refuge* (about 330 species recorded). The guide indicates stopping points on the 1.25-mile trail that passes through underbrush, a willow grove, and a young, planted forty-plus-year-old forest. The path circles West Pond (forty-five acres) and borders salt marshes.

The much less visited East Pond (100 acres) is located across Cross Bay Boulevard, and while the path to the pond is gravel, the encircling walkway can be muddy. When water levels are high, the path may disappear altogether. Venture on if you have waterproof shoes. The far side of the pond is quite close to the subway embankment, a curious juxtaposition between nature and urban transit.

If the day is young and the sun is still up, you might want to rejoin the subway at Broad Channel and head out to the Rockaways for a walk on the beach. For a full day of it, see Escape 10, "Beach and Boardwalking: The Rockaways East and West."

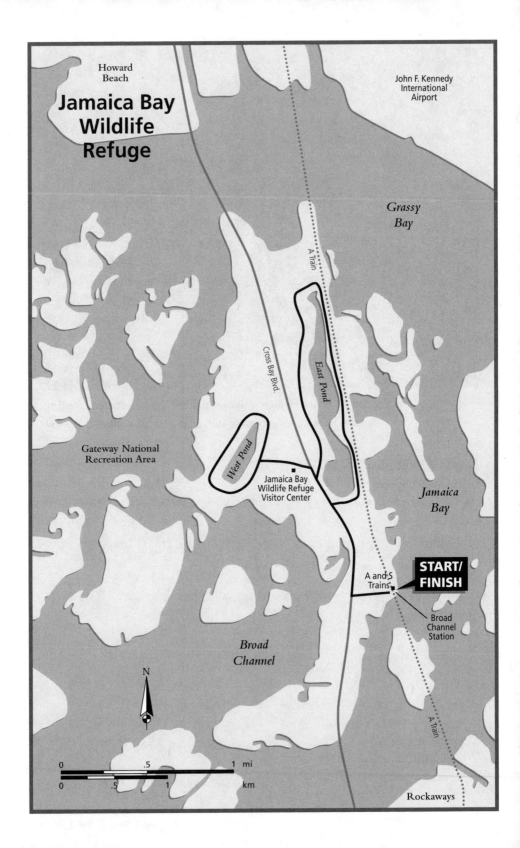

The Jamaica Bay Wildlife Refuge, a national urban park in the Borough of Queens, is a major stopover for birds using the Atlantic Flyway.

For More Information

New York City Transit Authority: (718) 330–1234; www.mta.info. Subway and bus information.

Jamaica Bay Wildlife Refuge: (718) 318–4340; www.brooklynbirdclub.org/ jamaica.htm or www.fieldtrip.com/ny/83184340.htm.

Gateway National Recreation Area: Floyd Bennett Field, Brooklyn, NY 11231; (718) 338–3799.

10 Beach and Boardwalking: The Rockaways East and West

An aboveground subway ride out over Jamaica Bay leads to the Rockaway Peninsula, where there are sandy beaches both remote and popular, and one of America's longest boardwalks parallels the Atlantic Ocean. Cyclists can easily cover the entire Rockaway Peninsula stretching 12 miles from Breezy Point to the bridge over to Atlantic Beach. Swimming is best on Rockaway West at the Gateway National Recreation Area, where lifeguards are on duty in season.

Itinerary at a Glance

Starting point

Rockaway Park, Rockaway Peninsula, Queens, for both east and west journeys.

Travel directions to starting point

Subway: Take the A train marked FAR ROCKAWAY (*not* LEFFERTS BOULEVARD) from Manhattan, Brooklyn, or Queens stations to Broad Channel in the middle of Jamaica Bay. There, transfer to the Rockaway Park S Shuttle to the end of the line. To return from an eastbound trip, take the A train from Far Rockaway directly back to stations in Queens, Brooklyn, or Manhattan. Alternatively, take the Long Island Rail Road from the Far Rockaway station, leaving hourly, for Jamaica and Penn Station. From a westbound trek, you can return as you came—via the shuttle to Broad Channel and the A train. An alternative return, cutting off just over 2 miles eastward along the Rockaway Inlet, is the Q35 (Green Bus Lines— every twenty minutes on Saturday, thirty minutes on Sunday) from Beach 169th Street in Jacob Riis Park via Marine Parkway Bridge to connect to the #2 train (#5 Monday through Friday only) at Flatbush Avenue, Brooklyn.

Car: From the Belt Parkway, Brooklyn and Queens, exit south onto Cross Bay Boulevard in the direction of Howard Beach, Broad Channel, and the Rockaways. Park on the street (much easier outside of summer beach days). To return to your car from the east, take the Q22 (Green Bus Lines) from Seagirt Avenue and 20th Street (near end of the walk) to Rockaway Park. Service every fifteen minutes. From the west, you'll be returning on foot.

Bicycle: Brooklyn's Bedford Avenue, running south from the Eastern Parkway, has an on-street bike lane. Four miles south, turn left onto Avenue P (partly on-street bike lane) to Hendrickson, 1 block short of Flatbush Avenue, then turn right to Marine Park.

You might also consider taking the subway in one or both directions. One suggested route would be to take the #2 train (#5 weekdays only) to Brooklyn College, Flatbush Avenue, the end of the line (no permit required). The first 2 miles of Flatbush Avenue are very busy, but you can avoid some of this by turning left onto Avenue I, right onto East 56th Street, right onto Avenue T, heading across Flatbush 1 block, then turning left onto Hendrickson to Marine Park.

From Marine Park, an off-street path along Flatbush crosses Floyd Bennett Field and travels over the Marine Parkway Bridge to the Rockaway Peninsula at Jacob Riis Park. From here, you can go right on State Road to Breezy Point; or you can turn left onto a bike path on the Rockaway Inlet side, then turn right onto B145th to Rockaway Beach Boulevard and go left. At B108th, turn right to the Shore Front Parkway, which parallels the boardwalk. Bicycles are not permitted after 10:00 A.M., but the stretch after B73rd is so little used that there will be little interference from pedestrians. Approaching the built-up area of Far Rockaway, you might want to shift inland to Seagirt Boulevard. You can cut the ride short by following B13th inland, then angling left on Mott Avenue to the A train terminal for the subway-and-elevated ride back to Manhattan (no permit required). The more ambitious may continue to the bridge over to Atlantic Beach, the next barrier island. The nearest public transportation (4 miles east from the bridge) is the Long Beach Branch of the Long Island Rail Road for hourly trains back to Jamaica and Penn Station. (Permits required; see Appendix B.)

An elevated A-train parallels the beach and boardwalk along an undeveloped section of the Rockaway East Peninsula.

Difficulty level and special considerations

The Rockaway East trek is 7 miles, most of it on a completely level boardwalk, both wooden and concrete; there's some optional beach walking.

The Rockaway West trip is 13 miles, all on completely level boardwalk, mostly concrete, with stretches of beach and sidewalks. You can shorten this westward journey by a couple of miles if you don't make the complete loop.

Both walks are entirely out in the open, so have food and water and cover up upon leaving Rockaway Park for the boardwalk and beach. The best time to come, if you are not planning a day of swimming, is any fine day out of season. The ocean air and solitude will take you miles away from the big city. For the Rockaway East walk, a local street map will be handy, if only to find your way from the boardwalk to the Far Rockaway A train or the Long Island Rail Road terminals. It's only a fifteen-minute walk, but the street grid is a bit confusing. Directions will also be found at the end of the itinerary.

Introduction

The Rockaway Peninsula, located in southern Queens, is a relatively unknown part of New York City, except to its residents and beachgoers who flock to Jacob Riis Park and Breezy Point. The strip that extends east–west for 12 miles acts as a barrier island between the Atlantic Ocean and Jamaica Bay, the western end of which is part of the Gateway National Recreation Area.

Besides excellent sandy beaches, there are tight little communities such as the Irish-flavored Rockaway Park, streets of small summer shacks, some large project housing complexes, and a mixed residential area of middle class and low income at the Far Rockaway end, which abuts more upscale suburbs in western Nassau County.

The beauty of these peninsula hikes, Rockaway East and Rockaway West, is their access to the ocean. Most of the boardwalk is as wide open and tranquil a spot as you will find anywhere in the five boroughs. In summertime, some stretches of beach are crowded, but a few hundred yards farther on you may be quite alone for the next mile. You'll begin to wonder why this ocean-front property did not get built up like the Hamptons.

Historically, the Rockaways were a kind of nineteenth-century Hamptons, with homes and hotels for the well-to-do, but when the Long Island Rail Road laid its tracks to the South Fork's East End, the smart set followed. The middle class then arrived in the Rockaways, and the attractive communities of Rockaway Park, Belle Harbor, Neponsit, Roxbury, and Breezy Point remain much the same today. To the east, lanes and lanes of beach shacks appeared, and some pockets remain, but most sections turned into slum dwellings. In the 1970s, Mayor John Lindsay had hundreds torn down for an urban renewal project, but replacement housing has been slow in coming, and much of what was constructed is pretty grim given the outstanding oceanside surroundings. More recently, additional, higher-quality housing is being added. There is lots of contrast and wonderful stretches of beach to see as you walk or cycle either east or west.

Itinerary

Take the A Train! is the cry—but not north to Harlem. Instead, board at a Brooklyn- or Queens-bound platform and come to the surface in Queens to join a former Long Island Rail Road line that heads south past Aqueduct

Racetrack and Howard Beach, the stop for the connecting free bus to Kennedy. Suddenly, the train begins to climb a causeway; looking out the windows, you have the sensation of putting out to sea. Jamaica Bay, its marshes, and its islands are a major part of Gateway National Recreation Area. To the right, you will pass through Jamaica Bay Wildlife Refuge (see Escape 9) with freshwater ponds on either side. If you leave the train at the Broad Channel station, you can walk to the refuge entrance in twenty minutes and spend a few hours spotting all kinds of migrating and resident shorebirds.

For both the Rockaway East and West trips, Broad Channel is the transfer point for the S Shuttle train to Rockaway Park, while the A train continues to Far Rockaway. The shuttle arrives onto the peninsula, turns right, and the fourth stop is the end of the line. Out front, Beach 116th Street is Rockaway Park's main commercial artery, and you can top off your picnic supplies here at any number of places. Walking left, it's 2 blocks to the boardwalk and beach. On a clear day, you should be able to see Staten Island and New Jersey's Atlantic Highlands. The hikes and cycle routes now divide.

Option 1: Rockaway East

Turning left, you begin a continuous 7-mile boardwalk hike past low-rise apartments, a few projects, and some remaining beach shacks nearing Far Rockaway. But there are many long stretches with nothing more than brush inland and hints of where the roads were once lined with hundreds of summer shacks. At Beach 109th and 108th Streets, have a look at an original double row of shacks to see the way it was. At Beach 98th, Rockaway Playland opened in 1903, a rival to Coney Island; it closed in 1985, after which the place was leveled. Just inland, at Beach 67th Street, you will see Congregation Derech Emunah, a shingled synagogue (1903) that once was the religious centerpiece of a large Jewish community. Fire-damaged, it survives but certainly has an endangered aura about it. The beach is worth a diversion, but swimming is not recommended: There can be strong currents, and there are no lifeguards. After a long empty stretch and as you approach the built-up western edge of Far Rockaway, there are a few streets of original beach shacks in to the left.

Many more people are encountered as you enter Far Rockaway proper, with the tide often running fast through the narrow inlet between here and Atlantic Beach across the way. Midrise apartments give rise to high-rise, and the neighborhood improves at the bend in the boardwalk and along

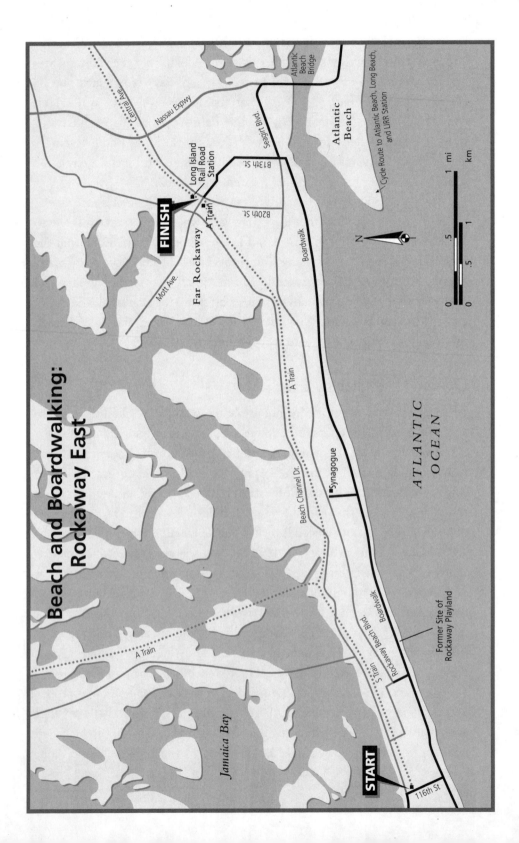

Beach and Boardwalking: Rockaway East

Jamaica Bay

Far Rockaway

FINISH

Long Island Rail Road Station

Central Ave.

Nassau Expwy

Mott Ave.

B13th St.

B20th St.

A Train

Seagirt Blvd.

Atlantic Beach Bridge

Atlantic Beach

Cycle Route to Atlantic Beach, Long Beach, and LIRR Station

A Train

Beach Channel Dr.

Boardwalk

Synagogue

S Train

Rockaway Beach Blvd.

Boardwalk

A Train

Former Site of Rockaway Playland

116th St

START

ATLANTIC OCEAN

N

0   .5   1 mi

0   .5   1 km

O'Donohue Park. You can reach Long Beach Island via a bridge than runs at right angles to Seagirt Boulevard, the first street in from the boardwalk.

For those who drove, you'll have to walk back along Seagirt to B20th Street, where the Q22 (Green Bus Lines) makes its turn to head west back to Rockaway Park. For the A train terminal, it's a fifteen-minute walk north on B13th Street; then angle left onto Mott Avenue. The LIRR terminal is 2 blocks to the right off Mott in a direct line from the A train terminal, but it may seem a bit hard to find in this rather dreary neighborhood. Take heart, though: If you're taking the LIRR train, the landscape changes immediately when you cross into more prosperous Nassau County. From the elevated A train, you get an aerial view of the route you took along the shore plus what lies inland. The ride back to Manhattan takes about an hour.

Option 2: Rockaway West

At the boardwalk end of B116th, turn right and begin the boardwalk-and-beach walk though Belle Harbor and Neponsit, two adjoining sections of small houses and narrow lanes to Jacob Riis Park, a 1937 Works Progress Administration beach and recreational site. On summer weekends, it will be very crowded here, with all types of New Yorkers enjoying a day by the ocean. The crowds disappear at Fort Tilden, where some defense fortifications and building remnants remain and nature is taking over. Opened in 1917 and closed in 1974, the fort's last significant use was during World War II with the threat of German submarines and aircraft. Nearly everything from Jacob Riis to Breezy Point, the western tip of the Rockaway Peninsula, is part of Gateway National Recreation Area. West of Fort Tilden, the beach is broad and inviting. Shortly before Breezy Point, you will pass what looks like a large motel, a summer complex used by people who rent for the season. On a fine day, this stretch of beach will be a family scene and largely Irish. The swimming is best here, and there are lifeguards in season.

At Breezy Point itself, you can walk out on the stone jetty to feel and see the full impact of the ocean waves. The jetty stretches north into the beginning of the Rockaway Inlet, and where it ends, the beach for the next mile is usually empty. Just inland is a nesting bird sanctuary. Rounding to the north side, you can usually stay on the beach in front of the Breezy Point community where families will be barbecuing and partying, but at some point you may also wish to cut inland to the boulevard to save some time. The road

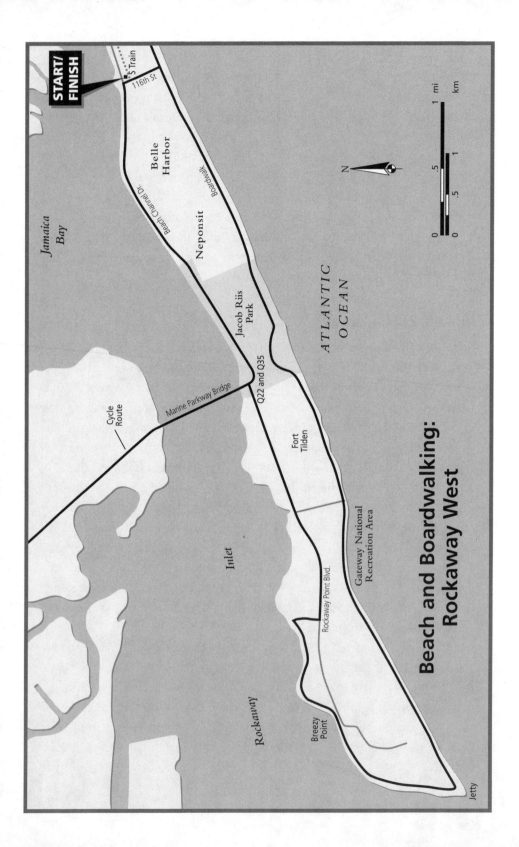

START/FINISH

S Train

116th St

Jamaica Bay

Beach Channel Dr.

Belle Harbor

Neponsit

Boardwalk

Jacob Riis Park

Cycle Route

Marine Parkway Bridge

Q22 and Q35

Fort Tilden

Gateway National Recreation Area

Rockaway Point Blvd.

Inlet

Rockaway

Breezy Point

Jetty

ATLANTIC OCEAN

N

0   .5   1 mi

0   .5   1   km

Beach and Boardwalking: Rockaway West

continues back into parkland, then runs straight and rather boringly between the small community of Roxbury facing Rockaway Inlet and Fort Tilden fronting on the Atlantic.

At Beach 169th Street, at the western end of Jacob Riis Park, you can cut the walk short by just over 2 miles by boarding the Q35 (Green Bus Lines) to the #2 train at Flatbush Avenue. Or continue walking through Jacob Riis, then along Rockaway Inlet's north side through Neponsit and Belle Harbor (site of the American Airlines crash on November 12, 2001) to the Rockaway Park station or to your car.

For More Information

NYC Transit Authority: (718) 330–1234; www.mta.info. Green Bus Lines Q22 and Q35 both take Transit Authority MetroCards.

Long Island Rail Road: (718) 217–LIRR; www.mta.info (Far Rockaway Branch).

Gateway National Recreation Area: (718) 318–4340.

Chamber of Commerce of the Rockaways, Inc.: (718) 634–1300; www.rockaway chamberofcommerce.com.

Staten Island Shoreline and History

This waters'-edge hike of about 10 miles takes in historic Fort Wadsworth perched high above the Narrows under the Verrazano-Narrows Bridge and the Alice Austen House, a charming harborside cottage owned by the noted nineteenth- and twentieth-century photographer.

Itinerary at a Glance

Starting point

Staten Island Railway's Oakwood Heights station.

Travel directions to starting point

Ferry and train: The Staten Island Ferry departs Lower Manhattan's Whitehall Terminal every hour on the half hour on weekend mornings until 11:30, when the service becomes half hourly as it is throughout the week. The ride takes twenty-five minutes. At St. George, Staten Island, follow signs to the Staten Island Railway, an aboveground subway-style train with the standard Transit Authority fare. The ride to Oakwood Heights (ten stops) takes about thirty minutes.

Car: It's best to park at the St. George Ferry Terminal on Staten Island, then take the SIR as above to Oakwood Heights. The hike returns to the ferry terminal.

Bicycle: The entire hike, apart from one short beach stretch (see the itinerary below), can be duplicated on two wheels. The Staten Island Ferry is free; board via the lower level. At St. George, wheel your bike through the terminal to the SIR and pay the regular passenger fare—no bike permit is needed. Ride out to the Oakwood Heights station and begin as with the hiking itinerary.

Difficulty level and special considerations

This 10-mile walk is easy but exposed with little shade, so a broiling-hot summer's day may not be the best time. It's a great brisk off-season walk at any time of the year. Bring food and water, as there are few places to buy either; there are, however, numerous places to stop, and some shady picnic tables to enjoy a lunch break. If you are interested in visiting the Alice Austen House, it has very limited afternoon opening hours (see below), but the grounds are open at all times. On certain weekends, there may be a wedding scheduled, and the house will likely be closed to the public. Also, crafts and collectibles fairs take place on the front lawn, so be sure to phone ahead. Bring rain gear if there's any chance of precipitation in the forecast. This is a wild-blue-yonder sort of day.

Introduction

Staten Island is the least-known and least-populated of all the five boroughs. Most people know it only from the ferry ride over and back, which is too bad. There are many places to visit, including the Snug Harbor Cultural Center for art, music, a botanical garden, a children's museum, and a wonderful collection of Greek Revival buildings; the Staten Island Zoo; the Jacques Marchais Center of Tibetan Art; and Richmond Town Restoration, a kind of very low-key Williamsburg.

While these sites are not along the hike, two other destinations are. Fort Wadsworth, now open to the public, stretches beneath the approach to the Verrazano-Narrows Bridge overlooking the Narrows between Staten Island and Brooklyn. The complex includes the longest continuously staffed military post in the United States; a wooden fort stood here during the seventeenth-century Dutch Nieuw Amsterdam occupation. There are batteries and fortifications to explore, but perhaps best of all is the wonderful view of the New York Harbor entrance and Brooklyn shoreline. Most New Yorkers have no idea that the grounds are now open to the public, hence there will be few others around.

The Alice Austen House, a tiny wooden cottage, occupies what must be the best catbird seat of any shoreline location. The house, originally built between 1691 and 1710, then Victorianized in 1846 with an additional wing, porch, dormers, and gingerbread woodwork, faces across a sloping lawn to Upper New York Bay and Lower Manhattan. Modest changing exhibits may or may not be of interest, but Alice Austen's life as an important photojournalist is worth the small admission fee.

The hike itself puts you in touch with both leafy-lane residential Staten Island and its wonderful coastline. The major portion of the route follows the beach, berms, dirt roads, concrete, and wooden stretches of boardwalk and offers sweeping views across Lower New York Bay to the Atlantic Highlands, Sandy Hook, tiny harbor islands, and seaside Brooklyn. The salt-air walk on a fine off-season day easily separates you from the hectic pace of New York City, at least for these couple of hours.

Itinerary

The twenty-two-minute Staten Island Ferry ride across Upper New York Bay is a delight at any time, with the Manhattan skyline receding in the wake, Governors Island to port, and Ellis Island and the Statue of Liberty to starboard. The ferries fall into three classes; one is named after Alice Austen, whose house is on this hike. In fact, four of the seven boats are named after Staten Islanders.

Docking at St. George, follow signs for the Staten Island Railway platforms. About ten minutes after the ferry arrival, the train is headed for Tottenville, located some 14 miles away at the south end of the island opposite Perth Amboy, New Jersey. Started in 1860 and completed to St. George in 1886, the rail line carried freight for the Baltimore & Ohio Railroad until 1971, but it is now solely used for passengers and is part of the MTA. The route affords a brief view of the harbor, but the ride is otherwise mostly suburban.

From the Oakwood Heights station, it's a thirty-minute residential neighborhood walk to the beach first via Guyon Avenue to busy Hylan Boulevard, then straight on. After 6 blocks, take a right onto Riga, go 2 blocks, then turn left onto Aviston and right onto Mill. Continue a short distance to Tarlton, then turn left onto one of three parallel roads leading to the dunes at Oakwood Beach. For cyclists, take Guyon Avenue across Hylan Boulevard, then continue straight for 7 blocks to Mill Road and turn left. Mill Road shortly becomes Old Mill Road and runs into Miller Field (see next paragraph). Join the hiking route at the far left-hand corner for the beach promenade.

Because of the water outlet to the Oakwood Beach Water Pollution Plant, you cannot walk right for any distance. The shoreline walk heading left is via a dirt road, a sandy path to a breakwater, then past the summer shacks at

Staten Island photographer Alice Austen lived in this Victorian Gothic Revival cottage, known as "Clear Comfort," for most of her life.

Cedar Grove Beach and along a berm then concrete road to Miller Field. Once part of William H. Vanderbilt's estate, then an air defense facility from 1919, this spot offers stark remnants of the military era. Now it's one vast series of ball fields, part of Gateway National Recreation Area and heavily used by sporting organizations involving all ages.

The continuous walkway, built in 1938, now runs parallel to Midland Beach and South Beach—once a rival to Coney Island, with Happyland Amusement Park, restaurants, tent colonies, and beach homes. Apart from a few comfort station structures (which may or may not be open) and some shady picnic areas, it's now pretty much returned to nature. Offshore, Swinburne Island once housed a crematorium; larger Hoffman Island was a quarantine station for immigrants with infectious diseases and a World War II training site. The inhabitants now are happy nesting birds.

Just before the boardwalk ends, with the Verrazano-Narrows Bridge looming ahead—two and a half to three hours after you first hit the beach— shift left to Father Capodanno Boulevard, which leads into Lily Pond Avenue as it swings left and uphill. Near the top, turn right onto Richmond Road

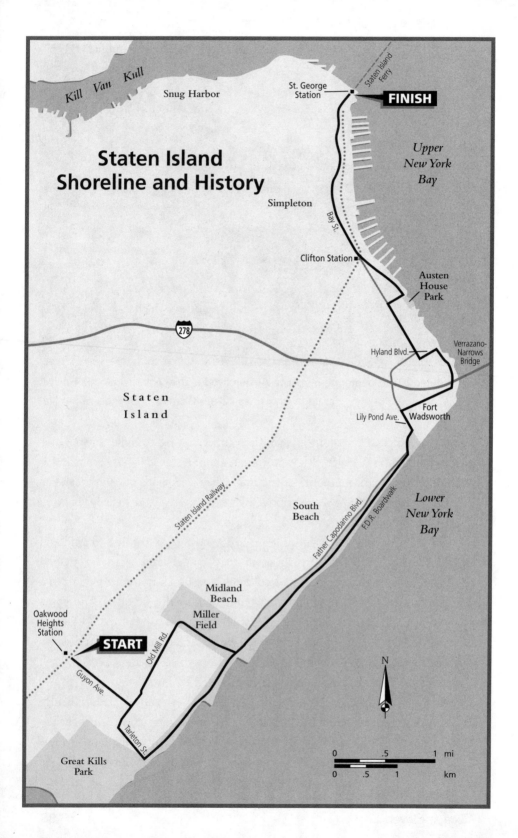

Kill Van Kull

Snug Harbor

St. George
Station

Staten Island Ferry

FINISH

**Staten Island
Shoreline and History**

*Upper
New York
Bay*

Simpleton

Bay St.

Clifton Station

Austen
House
Park

278

Hyland Blvd.

Verrazano-
Narrows
Bridge

S t a t e n
I s l a n d

Fort
Wadsworth

Lily Pond Ave.

Staten Island Railway

South
Beach

Father Capodanno Blvd.

F.D.R. Boardwalk

*Lower
New York
Bay*

Midland
Beach

Oakwood
Heights
Station

Miller
Field

Old Mill Rd.

START

N

Guyon Ave.

Tarleton St.

Great Kills
Park

0   .5   1 mi

0   .5   1   km

leading into Fort Wadsworth Naval Station, now open to the public, and follow the road that will swing left and pass under the dramatic bridge approach.

The Verrazano-Narrows Bridge opened on November 21, 1964, to become the world's longest suspension bridge (it's now the third longest), replacing a ferry that linked Brooklyn and Staten Island. Its construction changed the city's most rural borough forever, with an influx of new residents and expressways cutting a swath across and running down the length of the island as through-links between Long Island and New Jersey. The bridge towers are 623 feet high, and clearance for ships is 228 feet at mean high water—considerably higher than the East River bridges. On the north-side approach, there is a fine elevated view of the bridge span, Brooklyn shoreline, Manhattan across the bay, pre–Civil War Battery Weed below, and Fort Tompkins (1858–1876) behind. A line of interpretive plaques gives bridge and fort history. Linger a while, because you are enjoying one of the best views in New York, one few others have seen. Ships should pass below; on weekend afternoons look for a procession of cruise ships marching out for the Caribbean, Bermuda, New England, and Canada.

The fort road leads down to a line of military accommodations, and turns left then right out the gate to Bay Street. Wooded Von Briesen Park to the right is a favorite spot for wedding photographs with the bridge as a backdrop. Along Bay Street, you pass some Coast Guard housing and St. John's Episcopal Church (1871). At Hylan Boulevard, turn right and walk down to the shore. Immediately on the right is the Gothic Revival "Clear Comfort," Alice Austen's home from 1868 to shortly after the stock market crash, when she became indigent and had to leave.

The grounds are lovely and the interior modest. Gradually the Friends of the Alice Austen House are gathering more furnishings. Be sure to watch the video of her life and take in some of her photos, the collection housed at the Staten Island Historical Society. They depict social life on Staten Island, street life in Manhattan, and her beloved harbor out front.

From here you can walk back to the ferry terminal (forty-five minutes) via Edgewater Street, which begins at the house gate. Alternatively, where you join Bay Street, you can climb up to the SIR's Clifton station (trains leaving at about fifteen minutes to and fifteen minutes past the hour) for a three-stop ride to the ferry. The walk, neither scenic nor dull, passes near the docks and the former home port of the U.S. Navy, Bayley Seaton Hospital, and the old town centers at Stapleton and Tompkinsville, once important to the brewing

Battery Weed at Fort Wadsworth is the oldest military establishment in the United States, and it looks out to the Verrazano-Narrows Bridge and over to Bay Ridge, Brooklyn.

and shipping industries. If there is time before the ferry departs, have a look at the Staten Island Borough Hall (1906) and Richmond County Courthouse (1919), both landmarks facing the terminal, the new Staten Island Yankees ballpark, and the harbor. To the right of the terminal facing Manhattan, the National Lighthouse Museum is expanding within the historic buildings of a former Coast Guard base.

For More Information

New York City Transit Authority: (718) 330–1234; www.mta.info. Subway and bus information.

Alice Austen House: (718) 816–4506; www.aliceausten.8m.com. Open Thursday through Sunday, noon–5:00 P.M.; the grounds are open every day.

Council on the Arts and Humanities for Staten Island: (718) 447–3329; www.statenislandarts.org.

Fort Wadsworth: (718) 354–4500.

National Lighthouse Museum: (718) 556–1681; www.lighthousemuseum.org.

Staten Island Ferry Information: (718) 815–BOAT; www.siferry.com or www.nyc.gov/calldot.

Staten Island Railway Information: (718) 966–7478; www.mta.nyc.ny.us/nyct/sir.

Staten Island tourist information: www.statenislandusa.com/.

Staten Island Yankees: Richmond County Bank Ballpark; (718) 720–9265; www.siyanks.com.

12 Old Croton Aqueduct Trailway: Yonkers to Croton Dam in Three Sections

The Old Croton Aqueduct Trailway is the granddaddy of all level walks. The Westchester County section begins at the New York City/Yonkers line and threads its way north for 26.2 miles to Croton Gorge Park. The path cuts into the woods, marches over deep valleys on high viaducts, and passes through towns, across a college campus, and around human-made obstacles. Several historic houses and one significant museum lie along the fascinating route. The trailway is divided into three sections of about 9, 11, and 12 miles, but many other combinations can be substituted as outlined in the itinerary.

Itinerary at a Glance

Starting points

Section 1 begins at the Yonkers/New York City line or Yonkers Metro-North station; Section 2 at the Irvington-on-Hudson Metro-North station; Section 3 at the Scarborough Metro-North station.

Travel directions to starting points

The beauty of this hike is its ready access at many points along the Hudson Line of the Metro-North Railroad between Yonkers and Croton-Harmon, as well as an easy approach to its southern boundary with New York City. Because the full route is far too long to travel comfortably in a single day, the description will outline various stretches that can make up three or more individual walks. For Section 1, access will be by subway and bus or Metro-North train; for Sections 2 and 3, by Metro-North train. (See specific sections for access instructions including car approaches.)

Metro-North trains leave Grand Central Terminal in a distinct pattern: One hourly local train makes all stops, and one hourly express train calls at four trailway access points—Yonkers, Tarrytown, Ossining, and Croton-Harmon. With the exception of Croton-Harmon, the stations are no more than five to fifteen minutes on foot from the official trailway. In order not to backtrack, you can begin at one station, walk as far as you want, and return from another. Grand Central to Yonkers by train is twenty-five to thirty minutes, and Croton-Harmon, the farthest station from the city, is just fifty minutes. Starting or ending stations listed in the itinerary section are Yonkers, Irvington (local station), Scarborough (local station), and Croton-Harmon.

Bus: While there are Westchester County buses that parallel the trailway, the train is much faster and its Hudson River water-level vistas far more scenic.

Car: On weekends, you can easily park at any station, take the hike, and return to your car by train in a few minutes.

Difficulty level and special considerations

The hike, divided into stretches of similar lengths, is mostly flat, because the trail runs atop a gravity-flow aqueduct. There are a few climbs or descents where the route is blocked by modern intrusions, but nearly all are short. The path is grassy, dirt, gravel, and occasionally paved, and brief sections may be muddy after rain. Tall grass, until cut, is another concern in a few places because it may harbor the ticks that transmit Lyme disease, but it is always possible to walk around these patches. The best time to hike is when the leaves are off the trees and the river and distant landscapes are visible. Walking through wooded sections while they're shady may leave you feeling like you're walking through a tunnel after a few miles. Fall foliage is beautiful, but again, there are better ways to see the wooded landscape than being in the woods themselves. There are a few comfort stations along the way, most attached to a park or site you might visit. Bring water and food; there are numerous fine places to stop for a picnic. The path occasionally passes close to stores where you can buy food or top up your supplies.

Introduction

Considered one of the great engineering feats of the nineteenth century, the 41-mile Croton Aqueduct today hosts one of the most intriguing walks in the state. Completed in 1842 using Assyrian and Roman technology, the aqueduct solved New York City's water supply problems and gave its citizens ample fresh water for drinking, washing, cleaning the streets, and fighting fires in a wooden city. John B. Jervis, its chief engineer, had made his reputation building the Erie Canal, Delaware & Hudson Canal, and Mohawk & Hudson Railroad.

The water collected in the Croton Reservoir, a 5-mile-long lake created behind the Croton Dam, located 6 miles above the junction of the Croton and Hudson Rivers. A masonry aqueduct passed over the land, was buried in tunnels, and was catapulted over valleys on a landfill or arched structures. The aqueduct crossed from the Bronx into Upper Manhattan via the High Bridge; the water was stored in the Yorkville Receiving Reservoir—now the Great Lawn in Central Park—and distributed from the Murray Hill Reservoir, the present site of Bryant Park and the New York Public Library at 42nd Street and Fifth Avenue.

As the city grew, a second and much larger Croton Dam and Aqueduct were constructed beginning in the 1880s, and gradually the original aqueduct was taken out of service. In 1968, a 33-mile corridor atop the aqueduct was bought by New York State, and in 1974, the linear state park was added to the National Register of Historic Places. While the path is largely intact, some prior development and a few roadworks severed the pipe and occupied the land atop, making for some intriguing diversions, most of them brief.

With little staff assigned to the park, general maintenance is fair, but some sections are well used by locals for biking, jogging, and walking the dog. The trailway is not widely known outside local neighborhoods, yet a day's walk provides a fascinating kaleidoscope of urban, suburban, and rural landscapes; views of the Hudson Valley; and access to some amazing stone structures.

A hike may be combined with visits to Historic Hudson Valley properties such as Washington Irving's Sunnyside, Philipsburg Manor and Van Cortlandt Manor, the National Trust's Lyndhurst Castle, and Yonkers's (Glenwood) Hudson River Museum.

Be sure to read Appendix A, "Hudson River Rail Guide," if you are taking the train, and sit on the left side for the river views.

Itinerary

The routes suggested here begin in Yonkers (Section 1), Irvington (Section 2), and Scarborough (Section 3). The mileage figures begin from each station, and they are approximate, allowing for some short diversions.

Section 1: Yonkers to Irvington

There are two starting points here, one for purists who want to cover the entire trailway within Westchester County, the other for those who, perhaps after reading the description, would prefer to start at the Yonkers Metro-North station. The aqueduct path has walkable stretches within New York City in the University Heights section of the Bronx and a long, lonely wooded section north of the Jerome Park Reservoir in Van Cortlandt Park to the Westchester County line. Access to the wooded section from the south is alongside the Major Deegan Expressway and Mosholu Parkway, but this is not recommended unless you're in a group of four or more.

To reach the official starting point at the New York City/Yonkers line, West Siders take the Broadway #1/9 Local to the end of the elevated line at 242nd Street; alongside Van Cortlandt Park, take the Bx9 bus up Broadway to the end of the route at West 262nd Street, the Yonkers city line. East Siders take the #4 subway to the Kingsbridge Road elevated station in the Bronx, and then the Bx9 west to West 262nd Street and Broadway.

It's now 1 mile to the Old Croton Aqueduct Trailway. The hike begins by crossing up into Yonkers then taking an immediate right onto Caryl Avenue, which in 4 blocks makes a bit of a jog left, then right; then it runs into McLean Avenue. The winding road crosses the Saw Mill River Parkway. Just short of Midland Avenue, the trail runs right into Van Cortlandt Park in the Bronx, and left into a neighborhood of single-family houses. This is Yonkers's more affluent East Side. Almost immediately the dirt path meets one of the tall stone ventilation shafts, this one #24. The path becomes paved entering linear Tibbetts Brook Park, and at Teresa Avenue it passes through a stone

The Octagon House, built in 1860 and later enlarged, is a private home along the Old Croton Aqueduct Trailway in Irvington-on-Hudson.

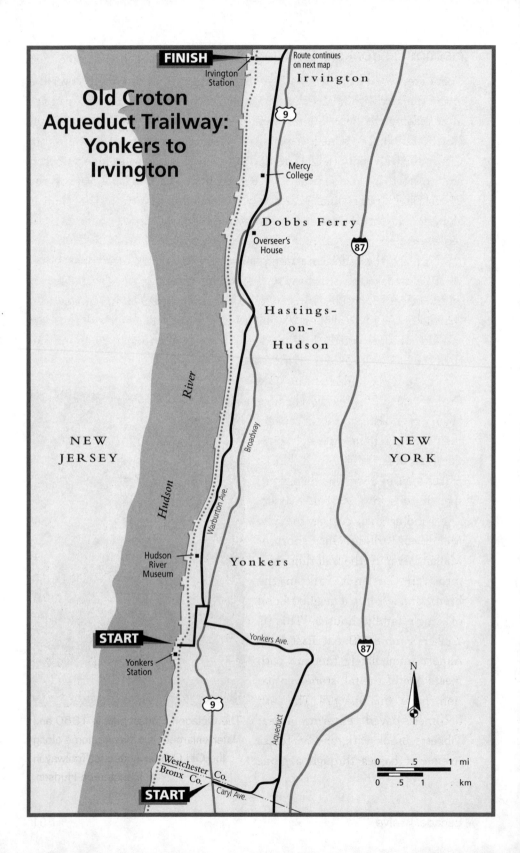

Old Croton Aqueduct Trailway: Yonkers to Irvington

FINISH

Route continues on next map

Irvington Station

Irvington

9

Mercy College

Dobbs Ferry

Overseer's House

87

Hastings-on-Hudson

River

NEW JERSEY

Broadway

NEW YORK

Warburton Ave.

Hudson

Hudson River Museum

Yonkers

START

Yonkers Station

Yonkers Ave.

87

9

Aqueduct

N

Westchester Co.
Bronx Co.

START

Caryl Ave.

0   .5   1 mi

0   .5   1   km

tunnel. It's just over a mile between stone vent shafts, and #23 comes just before the north end of the park, where the old aqueduct meets the new aqueduct near a stone water supply building.

The route becomes less attractive for a bit. It heads across the intersection and the left side of Yonkers Avenue under the Cross County Parkway, turns left to go under the old New York Central Putnam Division rail bridge (sections have become a cycle trail), then continues past the entrance to the Saw Mill River Parkway. At Prescott Street, take a paved path down to the right of Yonkers Avenue (vent shaft #22), rejoin the top of the aqueduct over Nepperhan Avenue, then continue on a wide arc past above the Yonkers War Memorial Field on the left. The neighborhood is shabby indeed. Before it seems to peter out, go right up to Ashburton Avenue, left ahead to Palisade Avenue, and turn right onto North Broadway. Turn left onto Lamartine Avenue and almost immediately right onto the aqueduct path, with the large stone ventilation shaft #21 dead ahead. It takes about forty-five minutes to cover the portion between the top end of Tibbetts Brook Park and vent shaft #21. The description from the Yonkers Metro-North Station joins here.

From Grand Central to Yonkers Station, the "Hudson River Rail Guide" will tell you what sights can be seen during the twenty-five-minute ride. For motorists, Broadway continues up into Yonkers; follow signs to the station. At Yonkers, the substantial former New York Central station sits close to the river and opposite the city's covered recreation pier, which once served Hudson River Day Line steamboats on their way between New York, Bear Mountain, West Point, Poughkeepsie, Catskill, and Albany. Walk east away from the river and across Larkin Plaza to Warburton Avenue, where on the corner is Philipse Manor Hall (circa 1680). The Georgian Colonial–style house belonged to the rich Philipse family, who owned and operated a huge regional estate north of here. Walk north along Warburton for 6 blocks to Lamartine Avenue, turn right up the hill to the Aqueduct Trail, and turn left. Vent shaft #21 is straight ahead. The route now joins the path followed by those who walked the 4 miles from the Yonkers border through Tibbetts Brook Park.

One of many cylindrical stone ventilation shafts, #21 was built to aerate the flowing water to maintain its freshness and prevent pressurization. These ancient-looking monuments were spaced roughly 1 mile apart, though a few are spaced 2 or 3 miles apart. From here, the unmistakable tree-fringed trailway runs straight between shabby buildings, although the neighborhood improves markedly within 0.5 mile as you approach the Glenwood section of Yonkers. At Glenwood Avenue, it's a five-minute steep walk down to the Glenwood station, also an alternate start for those wishing to avoid the urban nature of Yonkers.

Glenwood is home to Trevor Park and the Hudson River Museum, marked by a square Victorian tower down to the left sitting atop the 1876 Trevor Mansion. The several museum buildings house art exhibitions, Victorian furnishings, a planetarium, excellent children's programs, and outdoor summer concerts. Farther along, plain apartments rise from below, while substantial homes lie above.

Partly hidden in the trees, bas-reliefs of lions, a gate, and some steps mark the now ruined entrance to Greystone, the former estate of hatmaker John Waring that later served as home to Samuel J. Tilden, governor of New York. The curious may wish to climb the old carriage path to see the Grecian gardens, now a park with a splendid view over the Hudson.

The path continues into Hastings and arrives at a major intersection with Route 9, marked by the Carpenter Gothic Grace Episcopal Church (1867). It's 5 miles from the Yonkers station, 8 from the Yonkers city line. Cross with the traffic lights (two sets); the raised path continues to the left of a playing field (portable toilets) and enters Dobbs Ferry through a prosperous suburban neighborhood.

The Italianate brick house, set just off the trailway, was home to the aqueduct's overseer and occupied until the mid-1950s. The adjacent 1880s brown barn houses the trailway's maintenance equipment; the park's headquarters is housed in a trailer. For the Dobbs Ferry station (seven minutes), turn left onto Walnut Street and walk down to the river. When the path arrives at a parking lot, simply continue straight ahead to Cedar Street. Around the corner to the left is Dobbs Ferry's Main Street, with a couple of restaurants and stores to buy food and drinks.

Across Cedar Street from a little park, the path drops down onto the continuing aqueduct as it emerges from beneath the town. Soon the raised trailway mound crosses the Mercy College campus and enters the majestic parkland grounds belonging to Columbia University. Nevis, the Greek Revival mansion down to the left, was built in 1835 for Colonel James Hamilton, son of Alexander Hamilton (who was born on the West Indian island of Nevis).

Then left through the trees stands a colorfully painted Victorian Octagon House, built by banker Paul J. Armour in the 1860s and later enlarged to four stories. It's a private residence, but you can stand in the fringing woods at the property line or at the entrance to the drive to have a look. The neighborhood is now very well heeled. The aqueduct crosses a deep valley on a massive earthen embankment pierced down at the base by a country lane.

Just after vent shaft #16, the path arrives at Irvington's Main Street, which leads 0.5 mile downhill to the station (9 miles from the Yonkers station, 12 from the Yonkers city line). The attractive street is lined with antiques and collectibles stores, and useful places to eat and buy food. At the top end, the schoolyard has picnic tables. You've reached the end of Section 1.

Section 2: Irvington to Scarborough

Arrive at the Irvington station by train and climb Main Street; just past the school, the trailway crosses the street. Drivers should use Route 9 north and turn left onto Main Street. The trail crosses the street just before the school. Going right leads south to Yonkers and New York City. Go left, through the parking lot, and the path continues attractively through a leafy suburban neighborhood. At Sunnyside Lane, the winding road leads down to

Hikers traverse a wooded portion of the 27-mile Old Croton Aqueduct Trailway in Westchester County.

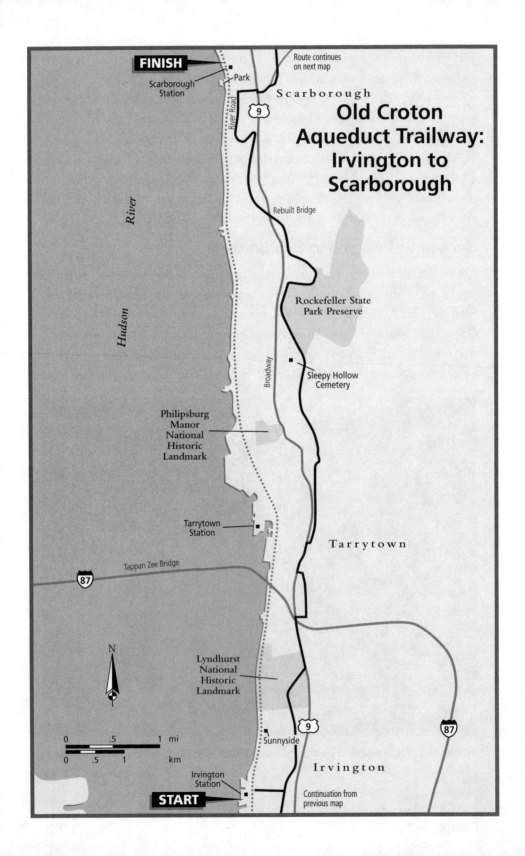

Washington Irving's romantic early-nineteenth-century estate, Sunnyside, one of the Historic Hudson Valley properties and well worth a visit.

The bordering line of trees soon gives way to the sixty-seven-acre land-scaped grounds of Lyndhurst, first constructed in 1838 and later enlarged into an American Gothic Revival–style castle. Erie Railroad magnate Jay Gould lived here, mooring his yacht at a dock on the river below to avoid using the rival New York Central Railroad just below his property. The National Trust operates regular tours, revealing an opulant way of life; afterward you can tour the gardens.

The Croton Aqueduct path marches straight across the Lyndhurst property amid majestic copper beech trees to Route 9, here called South Broadway. The sidewalk path crosses the New York State Thruway above the Tappan Zee Bridge toll plaza. Just after crossing the Thruway and exit ramp, turn right at this major traffic light intersection and walk five minutes up Route 119/White Plains Road. Turn left at vent shaft #14 and rejoin aqueduct trail for about 0.3 mile to Leroy Street. Turn left, then right almost immediately back onto South Broadway/Route 9.

If you wish to return to Grand Central, continue 0.3 mile along South Broadway, turn left on Main Street and walk 0.5 mile down the hill to the station. Tarrytown has both local and express service. Just a mile to the north, Sleepy Hollow Restorations' Philipsburg Manor, an early-eighteenth-century Dutch commercial center, offers tours of the manor house, mill, and small working farm.

The aqueduct path is again accessed 2 blocks before Main Street, Tarrytown, by turning right onto East Franklin then, just up the hill, turning left at vent shaft #13. The trail slices between houses until it rises to a high embankment leaving town. Soon a glass structure connecting two sections of Sleepy Hollow High School lies across the path. On weekdays you can walk straight through, but on weekends the doors are locked, and you must drop down to the right of the school and then climb up again to the faculty parking lot. On the far side, the path resumes in earnest.

The wooded path clings to the hillside high above Douglas Park and Sleepy Hollow Cemetery before swinging left over the Pocantico River at a point where the Headless Horseman is said to have scared Ichabod Crane. The trail now doubles as a bridle path. At an iron bridge crossing Route 177, a second path leads into Rockefeller State Park Preserve, with more extensive trails to explore.

The trail passes vent shaft #11 and angles left on a relatively new alignment that uses a rebuilt (formerly Archville) bridge over busy Broadway/Route 9 into Rockwood Hall, a former William Rockefeller Estate. The wide path continues for 0.3 mile to median-divided Country Club Road. Unlikely as it first may seem, you should walk straight across into a very narrow opening with a yellow clapboard house appearing just to the left. Proceed straight onto Route 9, where the aqueduct crosses the busy road into the woods. Hikers, however, must now take a long (but not uninteresting) detour via River Road, then a shortcut right on Creighton Road, to rejoin River Road. There are now great Hudson River views between the houses. Just short of the Scarborough station, cross the tracks via a bridge to a small riverside park for a splendid picnic spot with views up and down the Hudson and of approaching Metro-North and Amtrak trains. Scarborough is a local station with hourly weekend service; it's 9 miles from Irvington and the end of Section 2. The inbound platform could not be sited any closer to the river—a very cold place to stand in winter.

Section 3: Scarborough to Croton Dam to Croton-Harmon

Riding from Grand Central to Scarborough takes just under an hour on the local train. For drivers using Route 9, take a left onto Scarborough Station Road; it's 0.3 mile to the station.

Walk south from the station to the junction of River Road (for the route south) and Scarborough Station Road. Turn left and walk straight inland, cross Route 9 opposite a Presbyterian church, and continue on until you see the rounded aqueduct mound. Go left into the woods, passing vent shaft #9. The aqueduct veers left into Ossining, crosses Route 9, passes at an angle through two small parks, and, at vent shaft #8, bears right onto Spring Street.

Spring runs into Ossining's Main Street and an impressive row of late-nineteenth-century commercial buildings. Left on Main, it's 0.5 mile down to Ossining Station (local and express service). The trail crosses Main, slices on a brick surface between buildings, and arrives at one of the aqueduct's most dramatic structures, the stone-arched aqueduct over Sing Sing Creek. Built in 1839, it can be best viewed by dropping to the viewing platform on the left side just before crossing it. On the opposite side, the Double Arch Weir (tours by appointment) has steps within that lead down into the aqueduct tunnel. Excess water could be drawn off into Sing Sing Creek.

On the far side, the trail climbs up and down through a small park, past a

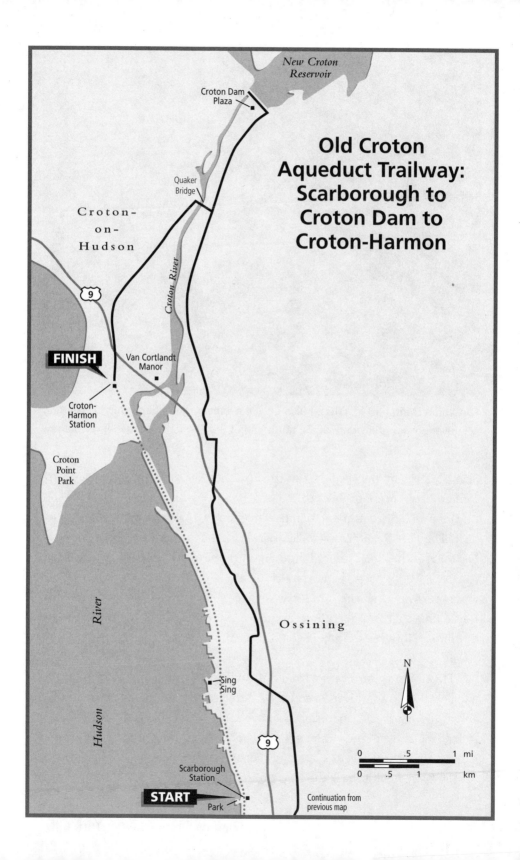

New Croton
Reservoir

Croton Dam
Plaza

**Old Croton
Aqueduct Trailway:
Scarborough to
Croton Dam to
Croton-Harmon**

Quaker
Bridge

Croton–
on–
Hudson

Croton River

9

FINISH

Van Cortlandt
Manor

Croton-
Harmon
Station

Croton
Point
Park

River

Ossining

Hudson

Sing
Sing

9

N

0   .5   1 mi

0   .5   1 km

Scarborough
Station

START

Park

Continuation from
previous map

Croton Dam, built in 1907, holds back the waters of the Croton Reservoir and overlooks a pretty park at the north end of the Old Croton Aqueduct Trailway.

Spanish-style firehouse (left), and on to another crossing of Route 9. At Ogden Road, turn left down to the Old Albany Post Road, then right. If you continue straight, you come to impassable Route 9A, which severed the aqueduct. The Post Road passes a Victorian brick lodge and a redbrick American Legion Hall then goes under Route 9A. Just ahead and slightly right, a small CROTON AQUEDUCT sign leads you up to the right of the road and left of the fence surrounding the property of the General Electric Management Development Institute. Follow the fence; the path angles right and drops down to an intersection where you will see the aqueduct trail stretching away ahead.

The trail now turns away from the Hudson and, on a high embankment, parallels the Croton River (seen below through the woods). When the leaves are off the trees, you can look back along the little river to the larger Hudson. It is now just over 2 miles along a wide wooded path that crosses a couple of roads, passes the last vent shaft, and then ends with the dramatic sight of the Croton Dam, holding back the New Croton Reservoir. Rising 200 feet above a pretty park, the stone structure was built by Italian stonemasons in 1907. Water cascades, depending on the season, over a stepped spillway on the far left side. View the reservoir from the road over the dam, then drop down the steep slope to Croton Gorge Park with picnic tables and rest rooms. It is an ideal spot for a picnic. It's 8 miles from the Scarborough station, and 3 miles to Croton-Harmon.

To return to the nearest Metro-North station, Croton-Harmon, climb back up to the trail and retrace your steps for 1 mile to Quaker Bridge Road. Turn down the winding road to the charming Quaker Bridge (1894) spanning the Croton River. Immediately after reaching the far side, turn left up into the woods along a narrow path that climbs to some tennis courts and a parking lot. Continuing ahead, you begin to enter leafy Croton-on-Hudson; even if you miss a turn here and there, you won't be lost for long. Walk along Truesdale Drive, continue across the first sloping intersection to Arlington Drive, and angle left to Devon Avenue; then turn right onto Young and left onto Benedict Boulevard to a commercial corner. It's a thirty-minute walk to this point from the parking lot. Go left down the hill on South Riverside and right at the RAIL-ROAD STATION sign, under Route 9/9A, then left down into the vast Croton-Harmon station parking lot (3 miles from Croton Dam, 11 miles from the Scarborough station, 27 miles from the Yonkers station, 30 miles from the Yonkers/New York City line). The local train starts at Croton-Harmon, but take the express. Both are reached by taking the overhead enclosed bridge to the same platform. The express takes fifty minutes and the local sixty-five minutes to Grand Central.

There is one more diversion if it's not too late in the day. Before turning right off South Riverside, walk straight; in five minutes, you'll reach Sleepy Hollow Restorations' Van Cortlandt Manor, a complex that depicts life between 1750 and 1815 with a handsome manor house, kitchen, ferry house (built next to the Croton River crossing), orchards, and gardens. Tucked away from the commercial sprawl and railroad, it is another world and well worth a visit.

For More Information

Metro-North Railroad, Hudson Line: (212) 532–4900 or (800) METRO–INFO; www.mta.info.

New York City Transit Authority: (718) 330–1234; www.mta.info. Subway and bus information.

Westchester County Bee-Line Bus: (914) 813–7777; www.beelinebus.com/.

Old Croton Trailway State Park: 15 Walnut Street, Dobbs Ferry, NY 10522; (914) 693–5259. Friends of Old Croton Aqueduct sell detailed full-color maps for $5.50. Write to the listed address.

Links to trailway and historic river towns of Westchester: www.hudson river.com.

New York State Parks, Recreation and Historic Preservation: www.nys parks.state.ny.us/.

Historic Hudson Valley: (914) 631–8200; www.hudsonvalley.org. Information on Sunnyside (Irvington), Lyndhurst (between Irvington and Tarrytown), Philipsburg Manor (Sleepy Hollow, just north of Tarrytown), Kykuit (the Rockefeller estate), and Van Cortlandt Manor (Croton-on-Hudson); links to Philipse Manor (Yonkers) and the Hudson River Museum (Glenwood, Yonkers).

13 Bear Mountain

Bear Mountain–Harriman State Park, located 50 miles north of the city and west of the Hudson, has 235 miles of marked trails traversing 52,000 wooded mountain acres, and is accessible by car, train, and bus at several starting points. The suggested 4-mile hike up 1,300-foot Bear Mountain serves as a good introduction to this vast wilderness. If you're arriving by train, add another 4 miles for the scenic route along the Appalachian Trail and across the Bear Mountain Bridge. Canoes, paddleboats, and rowboats can be rented at Hessian Lake in Bear Mountain State Park.

Itinerary at a Glance

Starting point

Bear Mountain Inn, Bear Mountain State Park.

Travel directions to starting point

Train: Metro-North's Hudson Line operates two morning trains, spaced about an hour apart, on a Saturday or Sunday (not weekdays) from Grand Central to the tiny hamlet of Manitou, located just above the Bear Mountain Bridge. Sit in the last car, because the Manitou platform is but one car long. The scenic ride takes eighty minutes (see Appendix A, "Hudson River Rail Guide," for a description). Two afternoon trains return from Manitou, spaced two hours apart, to Grand Central. The delightful walk from the station to the Bear Mountain Inn justifies including this means of access. When the train pulls away, you feel like you're being left in the middle of nowhere. Before heading to the bridge, cross the tracks to the tiny beach for a look across the Hudson and upriver to West Point. Take the only road across the grassy meadow, and where it begins to climb left up to Route 9D, turn right and follow a narrow upward lane, keeping mostly right, past some houses. In about ten minutes, you reach Route 9D. Ignore the signs saying PRIVATE ROAD (unless you're a noisy, intrusive group of one hundred). The alternative, staying left at the intersection, is not an attractive one, because you join busy Route 9D an additional 0.5 mile away from the bridge.

Walk on either side of Route 9D, and in 0.3 mile the Appalachian Trail from New England drops down onto the roadway. Shortly you come to the intersection of Routes 9D and 6/202. Cross to the left or south side to take the bridge's exhilarating footpath high over the Hudson. The Metro-North rail line that brought you here runs on the near side; the CSX (West Shore) freight rail line operates on the far side. The two-lane Bear Mountain Bridge opened in 1924. At the time it was the longest suspension bridge in the world.

Ahead, the flag flying over the Bear Mountain Inn should be visible above the trees, and low-lying Iona Island (a birding paradise) sits at a bend on the river to the left. After the tollbooths (no payment for pedestrians), turn left and follow the trail past an interpretive center for plants, trees, and animals to the level grounds laid out in front of Bear Mountain and the inn. Be sure to clock your walk from the station to the inn; you'll want to time your return for one of two afternoon trains back to the city. If you miss the last Sunday train, the next one is Saturday afternoon! You should allow about an hour from the inn to the station platform.

Bus: From Port Authority, take Route 2525. There are two morning buses up and two afternoon buses back (see "For More Information") directly to the Bear Mountain Inn, a trip of ninety minutes via the Lincoln Tunnel then northward on the west side of the Hudson.

Car: From the George Washington Bridge, take the Palisades Interstate Parkway directly to Bear Mountain, entering the park via the Seven Lakes Parkway exit or, from the north side, near the Bear Mountain Bridge entrance. From the city up the east side of the Hudson, take I–87, the New York State Thruway. Or you can parallel the Saw Mill River Parkway to Route 9A at Hawthorne until it runs into Route 9, then, north of Peekskill, follow Route 6/202 to the Bear Mountain Bridge (toll), crossing the Hudson to the park entrance. Parking costs $5.00 on weekends and holidays. The best driving combination would be to go one way up and back the other.

From Bear Mountain you can see down to the Bear Mountain Bridge and the Hudson River as it cuts through the Hudson Highlands.

Difficulty level and special considerations

Climbing Bear Mountain is a moderate hike if you're taking the Appalachian Trail (AT) up and down, or the Major Welch Trail down. The Major Welch is a more challenging climb up. When the leaves are on the trees, the views climbing Bear Mountain are obscured until you reach the top and go to the overlooks. Fall foliage is a great time for color but late fall, a warm winter day, or early spring is best for sight-seeing from the mountain. Bear Mountain is a cross-country ski area when there is snow; a skating rink also operates during the winter. In winter, the Major Welch Trail, facing north, can stay icy longer than the AT, so check before using this route. You will want to carry water, and bring a picnic or buy food and drink at the Bear Mountain Inn—which has good facilities for day visitors. You can also have a proper meal here and stay overnight.

This view from Bear Mountain is looking south along the Hudson Valley.

Introduction

Bear Mountain–Harriman State Park got its start in 1910 with a 10,000-acre donation to the state by railroad baron Edward H. Harriman and his wife, Mary A. Harriman. Subsequent additions brought the total to 52,000 acres, creating one of the greatest natural resources to be enjoyed so close to any major city. The park straddles Rockland and Orange Counties on the west side of the Hudson, all within New York State beginning just north of the New Jersey boundary. The northeast–southwest Appalachian Mountain ridges run through the park, and the Hudson Highlands are at their most dramatic on either side of the Hudson at the Bear Mountain Bridge. The Hudson River falls here to its maximum depth between New York and Albany, more than 300 feet. The state park is contiguous at the north end to the U.S. Military Academy at West Point. Getting to Bear Mountain is an integral part of the outing. It's best by train for the walk up to and across the Bear Mountain Bridge, or by car for the variety of approach routes.

The Bear Mountain Inn, built of boulders and chestnut logs, opened in 1915. It offers a full range of facilities for snacking and meals, a big stone fireplace, hotel rooms, lakeside lodges, and conference facilities. The inn is a busy place on a summer or fall-foliage weekend, and its park lodge ambience is best enjoyed in the off season. Out back, Hessian Lake has paddleboats, rowboats, and canoes for hire. Ball fields draw school groups. In summer the pool is open, and in winter there is cross-country skiing, ice skating, and sledding. The Bear Mountain Wildlife Center will delight the kids and city folks who want to recognize some of the area's fauna and flora. Because of the number of people on the main trails, it is unlikely you will see much wildlife beyond birds, squirrels, and maybe deer. You needn't worry about poisonous snakes, which tend to be very shy.

The New York–New Jersey Trail Conference's set of two maps— "Harriman Bear Mountain Trails"—are indispensable guides not only to the outing described here but also to the extensive network of trails that would take a month of Sundays to explore. Apart from the Bear Mountain Inn access, Port Authority buses serve the park's west side at Suffern, Sloatsburg, Tuxedo Park, Southfields, and Arden. New Jersey Transit's Main Line/Bergen County Line and its extension, Metro-North's Port Jervis Line, operate from Hoboken to Suffern, Sloatsburg, and Tuxedo Park. A trail starts from the Tuxedo Park station that makes possible half a dozen loop combinations.

Itinerary

Starting out at the Bear Mountain Inn, follow the white blazes of the Appalachian Trail, which swings behind the inn alongside Hessian Lake and heads over to the slope. The very first section of the Maine-to-Georgia 2,000-plus-mile AT was marked up Bear Mountain in 1922. The path heads into the wooded slopes, with occasional switchbacks, mixing moderate slopes upward with some ridge walking. The trail makes several crossings of a road built to give motorists access to viewpoints perched almost directly above the inn.

The trees are both evergreen and deciduous, so seasonal variations will produce varying good views on the way up. There are several viewpoints at the top with each facing one or more directions. The best view is from the Perkins Tower, named after George W. Perkins Sr., who was the Palisades Interstate Park Commission's first president, and a visionary and philanthropist. From the tower and other locations, you will be able to see West Point, the Catskills, the vast wooded expanse of the park extending southwest, and, best of all, the narrow Hudson Valley as it passes through the Highlands at the Bear

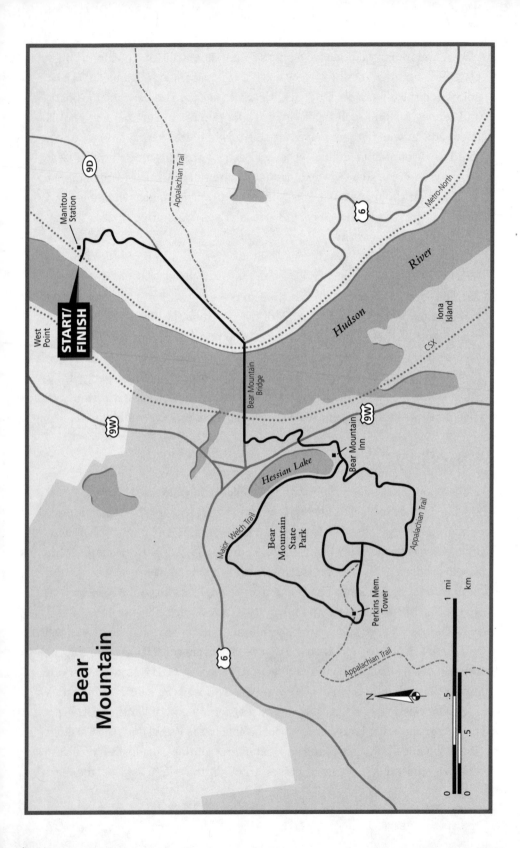

Bear
Mountain

START/
FINISH

West
Point

Manitou
Station

9D

Appalachian Trail

6

Metro-North

River

Hudson

CSX

Iona
Island

Bear Mountain Bridge

9W

9W

Bear Mountain
Inn

Hessian Lake

Major Welch Trail

Bear
Mountain
State
Park

Appalachian Trail

Perkins Mem.
Tower

6

Appalachian Trail

N

1 mi

km

.5

.5

1

1

0

0

Mountain Bridge and then widens on its way north. You may only be just over 1,300 feet up, but the grand view will make it seem much more than that. Rest rooms are available at the top. One drawback at the top is the presence of cars and motorcycles using Perkins Memorial Drive, but they have had less fun getting here.

The Appalachian Trail descends to the south and then west, a two-day, 20-mile hike to the edge of Harriman–Bear Mountain Park with campsites sited along the way. To return to Bear Mountain Inn, take the red-blazed Major Welch Trail (named after an early general manger of the park) heading away in a northerly direction, a 2-mile hike and a 900-foot descent. It crosses Perkins Memorial Drive, comes to a viewpoint looking north, begins a steep descent, then swings right to parallel Hessian Lake, intersecting with the Appalachian Trail near the inn.

For More Information

Metro-North Railroad: (212) 532–4900 or (800) METRO–INFO; www.mta.info.

Port Authority bus information: (212) 564–8484.

Coach USA, Short Line Bus, International Bus Services: www.shortlinebus.com/. See Appendix B for more details.

Bear Mountain Inn: (845) 786–2731; www.bearmountaininn.com.

Bear Mountain State Park Office: (845) 786–2701; www.hudsonriver. com/bearmtn.htm.

New York State Parks, Recreation and Historic Preservation: www.nysparks.state.ny.us/.

Appalachian Mountain Club: (212) 986–1430; amc-ny.org.

New York–New Jersey Trail Conference: (201) 512–9348; www.nynjtc.org.

It's worth spending a Saturday night in the Hudson Highlands, a rich destination for hiking and sight-seeing. There are two possible outings in this escape, first is a 7-mile ridge-and-valley hike into the Hudson Highlands from Breakneck in Dutchess County to the village of Cold Spring in Putnam County. There's also a 9-mile mountaintop-and-valley hike into the Hudson Highlands from Breakneck northeast to South and North Beacon Mountains, ending at the town of Beacon.

Itinerary at a Glance

Starting point

Breakneck Ridge station, Metro-North Railroad's Hudson Line.

Travel directions to starting point

Train: Two Metro-North morning weekend-only trains leave Grand Central for Breakneck Ridge, a highly scenic eighty-minute ride. Sit in the last car for the short platform at the Breakneck station. The first hike will loop south to Cold Spring for the hourly trains back to New York, while the second will go north and end at Beacon for hourly trains.

Car: The simplest route is to take the Taconic State Parkway northbound to Route 301W, then follow it to the traffic lights where Route 9D intersects with Main Street, Cold Spring. Go straight across and down through the center of town, then left over the bridge to the railroad station parking.

The more interesting driving route is to connect to Route 9A at Hawthorne from the Taconic State or Saw Mill River Parkway. Route 9A joins Route 9 at Crotonville. For a scenic final stretch, at Peekskill take Route 6/202, Bear Mountain Ridge Road; at the

Bear Mountain Bridge, angle right (north) on Route 9D. You then can look at part of the route for the hike up Bear Mountain (see Escape 13). Route 9D passes the turnoff to the Manitou station, the Garrison station, and Boscobel, the Federal-style restoration, before entering the village of Cold Spring. At Main Street (traffic lights) turn left down through the commercial center; just before the railroad tracks, bear left, cross a bridge over the line, and bear left again into the station parking lot. Take one of the two trains a day (see "Train," above) spaced about an hour apart for the four-minute ride from Cold Spring to the Breakneck station, the beginning of the hike. It is not advisable to walk these 2-plus miles, because most of the route is along very busy Route 9D then through a narrow tunnel. The first hike will bring you directly back to your car, the second to the Beacon station and the hourly trains back to Cold Spring. Alternatively, for the second hike you can drive through Cold Spring on Route 9D to the trailhead just north of the Breakneck Ridge tunnel and park your car there. There are, however, only two afternoon trains— spaced two hours apart—from Beacon at the end of the hike back to Breakneck station.

Difficulty level and special considerations

The first, 7-mile hike is paced at just over 1 mile an hour to allow for plenty of sight-seeing stops and the trails' hilly and sometimes steep nature. Anyone who is reasonably fit will be able to take this hike, and the truly athletic can do it at a faster pace. The start offers two alternatives: an easy bypass trail up to Breakneck Ridge or a direct scramble up the ridge's face. The route after that is the same. Once you begin the hike, there are no rest room facilities or drinking water until you reach Cold Spring. The trails are well marked and the itinerary descriptively detailed, but definitely buy a set of "East Hudson Trails" maps, published by the New York–New Jersey Trail Conference (see "For More Information," below).

The second, 9-mile hike covers similar terrain, and the alternative here is a steep climb up to South Beacon Mountain or an easier route around its base. You need to pay close attention to the detailed instructions so as not to get diverted from the route. Again, there are no rest room facilities or drinking water along the way. It would be wise to bring a trail map.

Introduction

The acquisition of land to form Hudson Highlands State Park began in earnest in the 1930s and continues to this day, creating a hiking region that is unmatched anywhere in the Hudson Valley. The Rockefellers, Whitneys, Nelsons, Wallaces, and Harrimans all contributed to the 4,200 acres we can now enjoy, and these are joined to adjacent conservation areas and private lands where there are additional trails.

Surprises await at almost every turn from mountaintop views down to the Hudson, east to the Catskills, and north and east to the surrounding New England states. In the valleys, you come across abandoned farmhouses and stone mills, left behind when the first wave of settlers pulled up stakes and moved west. The peace and quiet is magical, and there is a feeling of utter remoteness soon after the trail drops into a valley to follow a meandering stream. The rest of the world then no longer exists.

The trails are named and colored with blazes, either paint or plastic disks. The trails are maintained by volunteers who are members of the New York–New Jersey Trail Conference, while the park itself is under the aegis of the Taconic Region of the New York State Office of Parks, Recreation and Historic Preservation. The Scenic Hudson Land Trust, Inc., owns the Fishkill Ridge Conservation Area, which is integral to the second hike from Breakneck Station and another from Beacon. While there are two hikes described here, you can create additional treks, especially in Hudson Highlands State Park, covering entirely new ground.

The first hike ends at the village of Cold Spring, a delightful, mostly nineteenth-century community that is a mecca for antiques and collectibles. You'll also find restaurants and cafes at many different price levels, a couple of Main Street bed-and-breakfasts, and the Hudson House, a most attractive small inn and one of the only inns anywhere in the Hudson Valley that fronts directly onto the river, opposite Storm King and West Point. Consider lingering a while or even spending the night to enjoy more of the town and surrounding area.

The Federal-style Boscobel Restoration is a half-hour walk from Cold Spring and offers both a personal look into the life of the wealthy Dyckman family and a classic Hudson River view south to where the Highlands cross and form a part of Bear Mountain–Harriman State Park. (See Escape 13, "Bear Mountain.")

The second hike ends at Beacon, which has little to offer the visitor except for a few collectibles stores as you pass through the town en route to the river and the station.

Itinerary

Option 1: Breakneck Ridge to Cold Spring

The easier Breakneck By-Pass trail begins just south of the station or north of the Breakneck Tunnel at the point where the overhead wires cross Route 9D. The start is actually along the Wilkinson Memorial Trail, marked by a triple yellow blaze and named after Samuel N. Wilkinson, a tireless trail worker. The path climbs through the woods and crosses a brook. About ten minutes into the walk, the red-blazed Breakneck By-Pass trail goes off to the right and up a fairly steep ridge. The first viewpoint is next to a gullied woods road; you'll reach the top of the ridge about an hour after setting out. Onward and just below, you intersect with the main white-blazed Breakneck Ridge Trail.

The much steeper approach to the ridge itself is the white-blazed Breakneck Ridge Trail, which starts from Route 9D just north of the tunnel. Parking is off the road, and the Breakneck station is 0.5 mile farther along. It's a scramble and a very popular one, so you will have company—especially if you came up by train, because everyone starts out at once. The distance to the trail junction with the bypass route is just over a mile. There are three outstanding viewpoints near and at the top of the ridge.

Now with both routes converging, you aim northeast with another all-directions view. In 0.25 mile, intersect with the blue-blazed Notch Trail, which joins the Breakneck Ridge Trail. Turn right onto the Notch Trail. Descend steeply at first, then more gradually to a pond (left). The trail is now the old Lake Surprise Road, shaded by tall trees leading to the former dairy farm of Edward G. Cornish, once the owner and chairman of the National Lead Company. The main house was destroyed by fire in the 1920s, but stone farm building ruins remain. The red-blazed Brook Trail continues straight and then down to Route 9D, while the blue-blazed Notch Trail turns left, crosses the brook, enters a valley meadow, then begins to climb steeply up. About forty-five minutes later, you arrive at a four-way junction.

The blue-blazed Highland Trail heads southeast to Highland Road, while to the right an old wagon road zigzags to the summit of Mount Taurus (Bull Hill) where, a hundred years ago, a hotel had been planned but was never

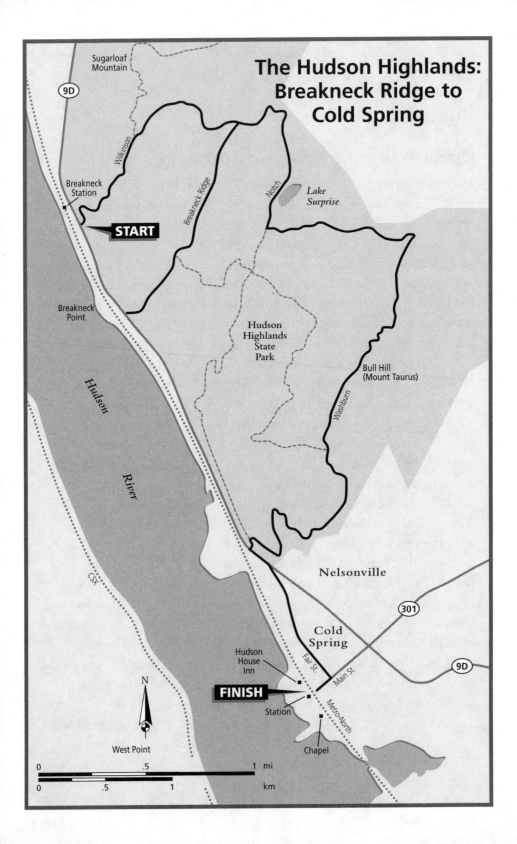

Hikers picnic atop Breakneck Ridge in Hudson Highlands.

completed. Continue straight, following the white-blazed Washburn Trail, which crosses the wagon road a couple of times on its way to the top. From the 1,400-foot peak, and as you walk westward, there are terrific views of the Highlands. It's almost 2 miles back to Route 9D, with additional viewpoints on the way down. The yellow-blazed Undercliff Trail heads down off to the right, and shortly thereafter an abandoned trail slopes down into Nelsonville, a village that is contiguous with Cold Spring.

At one point before the final descent, there is a view almost straight down to the river and Little Stony Point, a piece of land that juts into the Hudson. The Washburn Trail now passes along the rim of an old quarry, then across an overgrown field and into a relatively young forest. Arriving at busy Route 9D, it's just 200 yards south to Fair Street angling right and giving a much quieter approach to Cold Spring. It's less than fifteen minutes to Main Street and twenty to the station. If there is time before the train, walk down to the gazebo and river landing or walk to a knoll behind the station parking lot where a tiny Catholic chapel sits overlooking the river, a favorite location for weddings. The Hudson House, an attractive inn (1832) with rooms, a bar lounge, and a very good restaurant, sits facing the river opposite the gazebo. Have a look inside; you may wish to return for a weekend and more trail hiking.

Option 2: Breakneck Ridge to Beacon

This second hike is longer at 9 miles, and it's just about as challenging as the first—but it can be made even more so by the addition of climbing South Beacon Mountain, a little over halfway into the hike. The alternative is a gentler trail around its base.

Arriving train riders begin as above by walking south 0.25 mile to the point where the triple-yellow-blazed Wilkinson Memorial Trail begins. Motorists can usually park by the side of Route 9D next to the trailhead.

The Wilkinson Trail climbs fairly gently, crosses a brook, meets the red-blazed Breakneck By-Pass trail turning right and up, then diverges left from an abandoned trail, winding down to a stream and then steeply up Mount Sugarloaf (1,000 feet). The views are south to Breakneck Ridge and Storm King, west to the Catskills, north to the Beacon-Newburgh I–84 bridge spanning the Hudson, and directly down onto Bannerman's ruined castle on Pollepel Island.

There's another fine view five minutes on, then it's inland, first down, then up again alongside a brook and over it. About an hour after leaving Sugarloaf, without any stops, you come to a T junction where you turn right and up on a blue-and-yellow-blazed trail. Down left is also blazed with blue and yellow. In a couple of minutes, turn left onto the white-blazed Breakneck Ridge Trail. The path rises to Sunset Point then descends into a valley to meet the yellow-blazed trail coming in from the left. Now there's a major decision to make.

The harder route is a thirty- to forty-minute steep climb, even a bit of a scramble, up the white-blazed trail to South Beacon and its disused fire tower. There are great outlooks in all directions, including over the valley to the communication towers on North Beacon Mountain and to Beacon Reservoir down below. Leaving South Beacon, continue on the white-blazed trail down the far slope to its finish, then left along a dirt track to North Beacon. The easier route around South Beacon (see below) also passes the end of the white trail.

The gentler trail, blazed in yellow, goes straight ahead while the white-blazed trail goes left up South Beacon. In about 0.25-mile, the yellow-blazed trail veers right and up. Instead, follow an unmarked stony trail gradually up around the base of South Beacon, rising above left. Very shortly bear left on the same dirt track leading to the North Beacon communications towers. If you miss this turn, in another 0.25 mile you will arrive at the Beacon Reservoir, appearing on the left, and skirt it for another 0.25 mile until you arrive at the

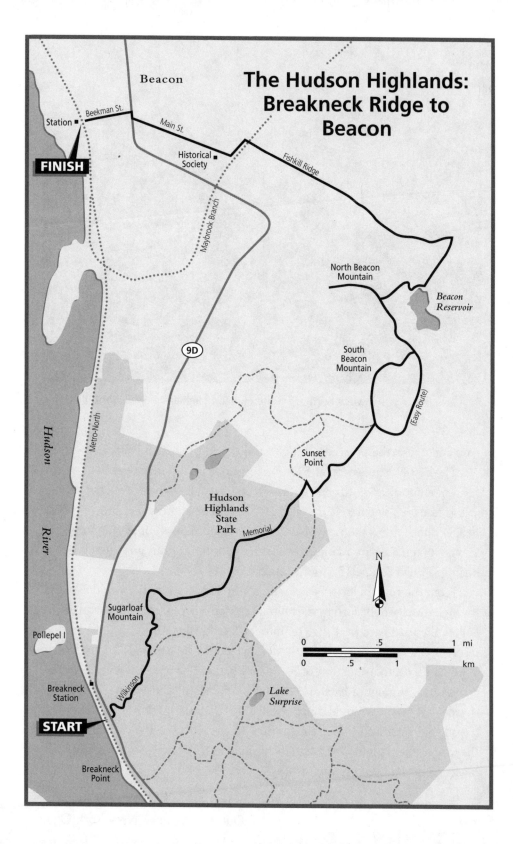

The Hudson Highlands:
Breakneck Ridge to
Beacon

Beacon

Station

Beekman St.

Main St.

FINISH

Historical
Society

Fishkill Ridge

Maybrook Branch

North Beacon
Mountain

*Beacon
Reservoir*

9D

South
Beacon
Mountain

(Easy Route)

Sunset
Point

Hudson

Metro-North

River

Hudson
Highlands
State
Park

Memorial

N

Sugarloaf
Mountain

Pollepel I

0 .5 1 mi
0 .5 1 km

Wilkinson

Breakneck
Station

*Lake
Surprise*

START

Breakneck
Point

A view north from the Hudson Highlands—well worth the hike.

dam and a road than runs down right, then up left to North Beacon.

The best North Beacon (1,513 feet) overlook is 0.25 mile beyond and west of the communication towers. On this site, the concrete platform once served as the base for a popular dance casino that overlooked the city of Beacon. Most people came up on the now abandoned inclined railway, operating until the 1960s, its remains are marked by the ruined top terminus and rusty mechanism. (See also Escape 15, "Mount Beacon.")

From the top of North Beacon, it's about a ninety-minute walk down and through the city of Beacon to the railroad station adjacent to the Hudson River. Follow the road back past the communications towers, then left down to the reservoir and dam. The now gently sloping gravel road descends for just under 0.5 mile to a minor junction of roads and paths. The choice is left down the gravel road, through a gate and left on paved Mountain Avenue, or slightly sharper left on the white-blazed Fishkill Ridge Trail alongside a stream down to a road that runs into Mountain Avenue. At the junction, the path ahead and the road to the right loop through the Fishkill Ridge Conservation Area, affording half a dozen good viewpoints. (Again, see Escape 15.)

Mountain Avenue, a neighborhood of single-family houses, becomes East Main. If you continue absolutely straight, it then becomes Spring; at Liberty, jog left near a Victorian firehouse then immediately right on East Main again. Cross Fishkill Creek and the tracks belonging to Metro-North's Maybrook Branch. Turn left and pass a former New Haven Railroad station, then turn immediately right, still Main Street, along a section of restored buildings, mainly propped up with antiques and collectibles stores and the local historical society.

It's then a dreary thirty-minute walk to the old center of Beacon just before reaching Route 9D. Cross 9D, jogging right and down through a sloping park (urban renewal area) to join Beekman, leading ever downward to Metro-North's Beacon station. If there is time before the train arrives, walk to the town park bordering the river and see the remains of the ferry slip used by the boats crossing to Newburgh until 1963, when the I–84 span (now two) replaced the ferry.

There are hourly trains from Beacon to Grand Central taking about ninety minutes, and just two that stop at Breakneck Station if your car is parked. Be sure to secure a seat on the right side for the river views. You have a good chance of doing so, because Beacon is only the second stop after Poughkeepsie.

For More Information

Metro-North Railroad, Hudson Line: (212) 532–4900 or (800) METRO–INFO; www.mta.info.

New York–New Jersey Trail Conference: (201) 512–9348; www.nynjtc.org.

Historic Hudson River: www.hhr.highlands.com. The site for the history, culture, and conservation of the Hudson River Valley with links to Bannerman's Island, Cold Spring Foundry, and the Cold Spring/Garrison/West Point area.

Hudson House: 2 Main Street, Cold Spring; (845) 265–9355; www.hudson houseinn.com.

Pig Hill Inn: 73 Main Street, Cold Spring; (845) 265–9247; www.pighill.com.

Boscobel Restoration: Garrison; (845) 265–3638; www.boscobel.org.

West Point Military Academy: (914) 938–2638; www.usma.edu.

15 Mount Beacon

This 8- to 10-mile hike takes you up a moderately steep 1-mile climb past the city of Beacon's water catchment reservoir and higher to North and South Beacon Mountains, the latter being the highest point in the Hudson Highlands. A 4-mile extension includes a Fishkill Ridge loop trail. The Beacon Mountain portion may also be visited on a Hudson Highlands hike from the Breakneck station to Beacon (see Escape 14).

Itinerary at a Glance

Starting point

Beacon station or the foot of the Fishkill Ridge Trail, at the east end of Beacon.

Travel directions to starting point

Train: Metro-North operates hourly trains from Grand Central and 125th Street up the Hudson Line to Beacon, a scenic ride of ninety minutes (see Appendix A, "Hudson River Rail Guide," for a description). From the station, climb on foot up Beekman Street to the intersection of North Avenue, turning right and then almost immediately left onto Main Street. The first part is scruffy then just a bit dull, but finally the handsome historical society and collectibles stores appear to dress up this end of town. At a former New Haven Railroad freight building, Main turns left for 1 block, then goes right across the Maybrook Branch tracks and Fishkill Creek. Stay on Main until it intersects with Howland Avenue, where it becomes Mountain Avenue. The road climbs gently through a suburban neighborhood and curves left. Just before the small bridge over Dry Creek, turn right and you will see some water tanks at the beginning of the Fishkill Ridge Trail (white blazes). Note that Parallel Reservoir Road (gravel) begins at Mountain Avenue just across this bridge—an alternate route, preferably downhill.

Car: Take the Taconic State Parkway northbound to Route 301W, then follow it until the traffic lights where Route 9D intersects with Main Street, Cold Spring. Go north on 9D through the Breakneck Ridge Tunnel (the Hudson Highland hikes starting point—see Escape 14) into Beacon. About 0.3 mile past the hospital, just as Route 9D curves left, continue straight onto Howland Avenue and continue to the intersection with Main Street and Mountain Road. Turn right onto Mountain and climb gently to just before a small bridge over Dry Creek. The water tanks just in to the right mark the start of the Fishkill Ridge Trail. Park where it seems legal; you may have to drive back a few blocks to find a space.

Difficulty level and special considerations

This 8- to 10-mile hike has a moderately difficult ascent of 0.75 mile, but most of the upward and downward slopes are gentle. The initial trail is narrow and can be muddy after wet weather. This trail up or down the mountain may also be avoided altogether by using the parallel Reservoir Road. After leaving the urban section of Beacon, there are no stores or rest rooms. Be sure to bring food and water—once you understand the geography at the top, you may wish to explore a bit farther than North Beacon Mountain.

Introduction

The Hudson Highlands are partly protected in a state park straddling Dutchess and Putnam Counties, and partly in Fishkill Ridge Conservation Area, located solely within Dutchess County. This area is laced with a few gravel access roads, which form sections of the route, but you rarely see any vehicles other than kids on ATVs, an annoyance when they are about.

Beacon Mountain took its name from a signal fire relay system that passed messages north and south along the ridges. South Beacon Mountain, the highest point in the Hudson Highlands, is marked by an abandoned fire tower, which will help guide you to the peak.

North Beacon Mountain was the site of a casino (entertainment, not gambling) and dance hall accessed by an inclined railway from the east end of the city of Beacon. The casino disappeared first; the incline lasted until the early 1960s, when it was abandoned. The route it took is still visible, however, as are ruins of the mechanism and brick station at the top.

The Fishkill Ridge loop is highly recommended for making a full day of it, with great additional views to the north and east. There is no backtracking.

The city of Beacon is largely low income in the center and middle class at the edges. Near Fishkill Creek, the city has some notable historic buildings, and the park fronting on the Hudson adjacent to the railroad station is a shady place to wait for the train. Just to the south of the park and west of the station are the rotting remains of a ferry slip that joined Beacon with Newburgh until I–84 was constructed in 1963.

Itinerary

The wooded white-blazed Fishkill Ridge Trail climbs steeply in places alongside Dry Creek; you'll need about forty minutes to reach an intersection with Reservoir Road. The Fishkill Ridge Trail goes left (see below), while the route up to North Beacon goes right via a gravel road. The road rises to the base of the reservoir, then right up past the communications towers and onto the promontory overlooking the city below, the Hudson, and west to the Catskills. The concrete platform shows the location of the casino; to the right is the incline's ruined machinery.

After taking in the view, consider following the ridge line for about 0.75 mile to the base of the South Beacon Mountain's abandoned fire tower. A white-blazed trail runs from the gravel road to the top and then steeply down toward Breakneck Ridge (see Escape 14).

If you can keep your wits about you, it is possible to descend from South Beacon, first on the route you ascended, then—instead of left, the way you arrived—go right and immediately left on an unmarked path that skirts the northeast side of the reservoir. You will join the gravel road that approaches the reservoir from below.

To take the 4-mile Fishkill Ridge loop, return to the junction with the trail you ascended, and continue straight on the white-blazed Fishkill Ridge Trail. Heading north, it ascends gently then sharply to a ridge for great Hudson Valley views. Lambs Hill is a 1,500-foot summit; the trail then descends to intersect with a woods road at a place named Dozer Junction, after the rusty bulldozer abandoned here. The trail follows a ridge to Bald Hill (which isn't), then soon makes a switchback, drops into the woods, and eventually joins a rough woods road, with the official Fishkill Ridge Trail ending where it meets

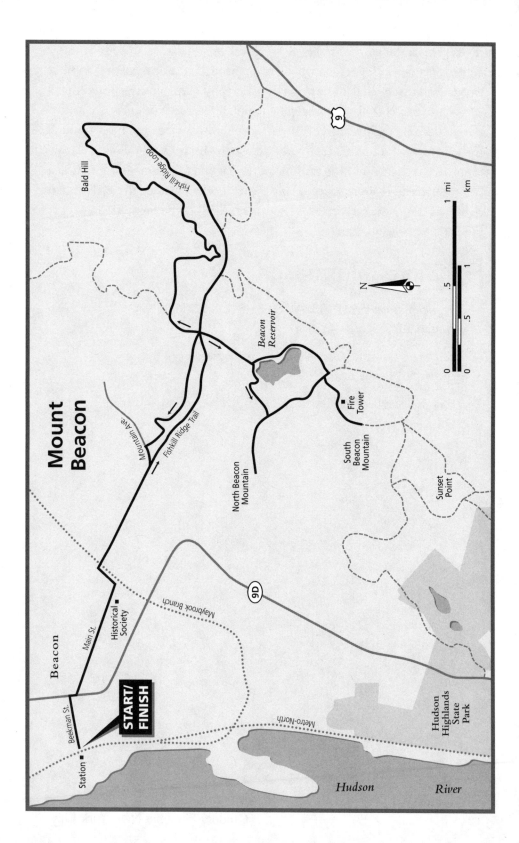

Mount Beacon

Beacon

START/FINISH

Beekman St.

Main St.

Historical Society

Maybrook Branch

9D

Station

Metro-North

Hudson

River

Hudson Highlands State Park

Mountain Ave.

Fishkill Ridge Trail

North Beacon Mountain

Beacon Reservoir

South Beacon Mountain

Fire Tower

Sunset Point

Bald Hill

Fishkill Ridge Loop

9

N

0   .5   1 mi

0   .5   1 km

the Wilkinson Memorial Trail (yellow blazes). When the Wilkinson turns left and steeply down, follow the woods road ahead as it drops, passing another woods road that goes right to Dozer Junction and then joins the Fishkill Trail where it intersects with the original junction and Reservoir Road. To avoid a repeat, descend via the road (sometimes stony) to a gate, and head through the gate to Mountain Road. Turn left, cross the bridge, and follow the same route back to your car or the station. Station-bound hikers may wish to take a street parallel to Main after recrossing the tracks then making the jog left then right past the historical society. If there is time before the train, have a look at the city's park facing the river.

For More Information

Metro-North Railroad: (212) 532–4900 or (800) METRO–INFO; www.mta.info.

New York State Parks, Recreation and Historic Preservation: www.nysparks.state.ny.us/.

New York–New Jersey Trail Conference: (201) 512–9348; www.nynjtc.org.

16 West of the Hudson Urban Waterfront: Jersey City, Hoboken, and Weehawken

This 7-mile hike begins in Jersey City, an old urban core under major renewal; continues through another being created out of an industrial landscape to the highly definable city of Hoboken; and finishes up with a million-dollar view from the Palisades across to Midtown Manhattan.

Itinerary at a Glance

Starting point

Exchange Place, Jersey City, across from Lower Manhattan.

Travel directions to starting point

Ferry: NY Waterway ferries leave from landings in Lower Manhattan sited at Battery Park City, Pier A at the Battery, and Pier 11, East River, at the foot of Wall Street. The ride across the Hudson to Colgate or Harborside, Jersey City, takes between five and ten minutes. Departure frequencies vary between ten and thirty minutes, depending on the time of day and day of the week. Ferries have temporarily replaced PATH train service from New Jersey, which was interrupted after the destruction of the World Trade Center. Full PATH service is scheduled to return to lower Manhattan in early 2004.

Car: Not recommended. A transit return from Weehawken to Jersey City is awkward and inconvenient until the waterfront Hudson-Bergen Light Rail Line is completed.

Difficulty level and special considerations

This hike ties together waterfront communities that have been around for 200 years with brand-new burgeoning neighborhoods still in the developing stage. Because the riverside locations had Manhattan as their raison d'être, none was very well connected to any others. Hence, a new street grid is being laid out where virtually no one had walked before. Taken as a whole, the outing presents a kaleidoscope of the old and new and an intriguing look into the future. There are numerous fun places to eat, so taking a picnic is not necessary; still, there are delightful places to have one by the river.

Introduction

The New Jersey waterfront immediately across from Manhattan first developed because of its proximity to the city, and because a river separated the two, there was need for transfer facilities. Exchange Place and Pavonia, Jersey City, Hoboken, and Weehawken all had railroad terminals and railroad navies for freight and passengers in among an almost continuous line of steamship piers. Industrial sites sprouted because of nearby transportation and the huge population as a ready market across the Hudson. Working-class housing got built to supply labor, and the industrial managers and owners lived in fine style in a few isolated pockets.

Beginning at the south end, just north of Ellis Island and the Statue of Liberty, stands the 1880s Jersey Central Terminal, a splendidly restored but now empty combination railroad-ferry terminal that connected the Central of New Jersey, Baltimore & Ohio, and Lehigh Valley Railroads to Manhattan via the Liberty Street Ferry until April 1967. The waterway to the north is the former entrance to the Morris Canal, now a marina, but the waterway once extended across the Garden State to the Delaware River and on, via other canals, to the Pennsylvania coal mines.

Exchange Place itself, where the walk begins, had a large Pennsylvania Railroad terminal that remained a secondary access to Lower Manhattan long after Penn Station, Manhattan, was completed in 1910. The various warehouses and industrial buildings that served the waterfront have either been pulled down or, like Harborside, recycled into new office space. There are still some hulking vestiges of the past—power plants and factories—sited a few blocks inland that have not yet succumbed to the wrecking ball and may see reuse.

Pavonia, now called Newport to give it more cachet, has completely reinvented itself. What were once vast railroad yards and cargo piers are now sites for a high-rise community of offices, chain hotels, and residences, with even a hint of a resort atmosphere where marinas and restaurants occupy the waterfront. It's a work in progress.

A New York Waterway ferry disembarks a cyclist and passengers at Weehawken after a trip across the Hudson from West 38th Street, Manhattan.

Hoboken is probably the best-defined community in the tristate region, as it has forever been hemmed in by barriers—the river, the Palisades, railyards, and a former swamp now occupied by the Lincoln Tunnel helix. Hoboken's isolation produced gradual development, from a ferry landing for New York, to an industrial port and residential city in its own right, to an almost purely residential community today, divided between those connected to the old Hoboken and newcomers for whom Hoboken is a bedroom suburb for jobs in Manhattan. Hoboken Terminal, one of the great joint railroad-ferry terminals in the world, is an architectural gem, and 14-block-long Washington Street is a step back in time to an authentic small-city Main Street, now poised between catering to the traditional working-class residents and serving the new, more moneyed younger crowd.

The outing finishes with a dramatic view from the top of the Palisades at Weehawken and an all-too-swift ferry ride back to Midtown Manhattan.

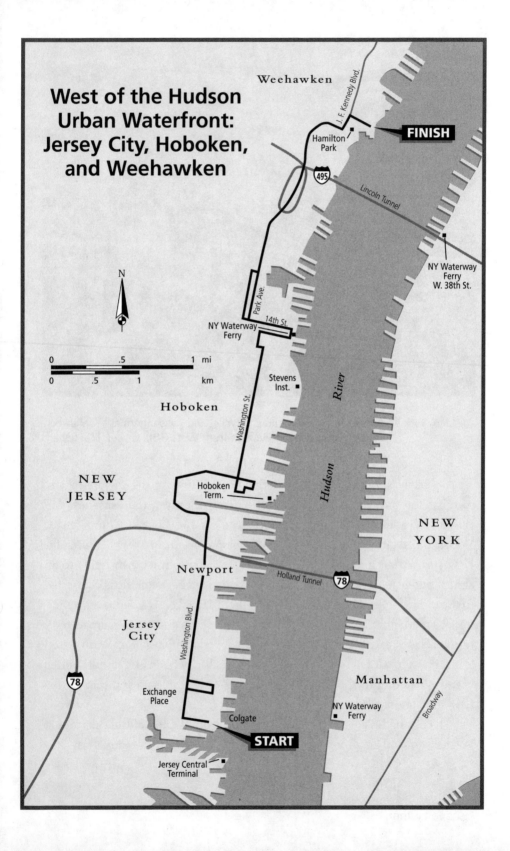

West of the Hudson Urban Waterfront: Jersey City, Hoboken, and Weehawken

Weehawken

J. F. Kennedy Blvd.

FINISH

Hamilton Park

495

Lincoln Tunnel

NY Waterway Ferry W. 38th St.

N

0   .5   1   mi

0   .5   1   km

Park Ave.

14th St.

NY Waterway Ferry

Stevens Inst.

Hudson

River

Hoboken

Washington St.

NEW JERSEY

Hoboken Term.

NEW YORK

Newport

Holland Tunnel

78

Jersey City

Washington Blvd.

Manhattan

78

Exchange Place

Broadway

Colgate

NY Waterway Ferry

START

Jersey Central Terminal

Itinerary

The hike starts in Lower Manhattan and crosses the Hudson by NY Waterway ferry to Colgate, the site of the Colgate Palmolive factory and next to a large lighted outdoor clock that sat atop the original headquarters. Some ferries land at Harborside just to the north, so walk the few blocks south to Colgate to begin exploring Exchange Place.

This area has been variously called Paulus Hook or Exchange Place, a part of greater Jersey City that extends for several miles inland and north to Hoboken. Two streets inland after you cross the Hudson-Bergen Light Rail Line, several square blocks of nineteenth-century row houses now qualify as a historic district. Gentrification is setting in because of the area's proximity to the new office complexes and to Lower Manhattan. Just to the south, high-rise apartments look south over the Morris Canal to Liberty State Park. Walking north to Montgomery Street, you pass buildings that exhibit an earlier period of greater importance, such as the block-long post office and the large Catholic church and school.

Returning toward the river along Montgomery to the intersection with Greene, the Flamingo Bar and Grill is a Greek-owned throwback to the 1940s. It's a lively combination bar, diner counter, and booth restaurant, packed at lunchtime with construction and office workers. You can't beat the atmosphere or the price of the meals.

At the waterfront plaza just in from the recreation pier, the statue of a bayoneted soldier marked KATYN 1940 commemorates the massacre of two million Poles and thousands of soldiers by the Soviets, a crime once blamed on the Germans. From here, follow the trolley tracks north past the Harborside Center and its ferry landing; when the tracks turn sharply left, walk straight through the gate marked AVALON COVE, a new high- and low-rise apartment cluster facing the water. A boardwalk skirts what used to be a cargo slip and leads into Washington Boulevard and Newport Center.

A long pier to the right serves the Newport Marina, restaurant, and cafe, and is worth a diversion. Ahead, you are hemmed in by an indoor shopping mall, office buildings, and chain hotels—an entirely new city built over an industrial landscape. A few bits of railroad heritage such as warehouses, transfer bridges, and tracks survive at the north end of old Pavonia, now Newport.

The Hudson-Bergen Light Rail Line rises from the street to an elevated concrete structure for its new route into Hoboken, with an extension into

Weehawken (reaching the NY–Weehawken ferry terminal in mid-2004) and through a tunnel under the Palisades to a station near the New Jersey Turnpike. Simply follow Washington Boulevard, which goes left along the rail structure then under it to turn right on Marin Boulevard. Continue north under the New Jersey Transit railroad bridges leading into the Hoboken Terminal. At Observer Highway, go right.

While the most direct route follows Observer Highway to the Hoboken Terminal seen ahead about a mile away, it's much more interesting to angle left onto Newark Avenue (Stevens campus sign) to 1st Street, then bear right through a low-rise residential neighborhood punctuated with tiny stores. First Street comes up past the backside of Hoboken's yellow-brick City Hall to Washington Street, the city's main drag. Turn right onto Washington then left onto Newark to visit the splendid Beaux Arts Lackawanna Terminal, a masterpiece of engineering and design when it opened in 1905. Watch for the opening of a shoreline path that will eliminate the less attractive inland route described here.

Built to accommodate the Lackawanna Railroad's long-distance and suburban trains, local trolley lines, vehicular traffic, and three Lackawanna ferry routes to Manhattan from six slips, an ingenious floor plan handled the daily flow of 100,000 passengers. The terminal's decorative features include an elaborately crafted copper exterior and a 50-foot-high iron-and-limestone-accented waiting room, lighted by a Tiffany glass skylight, massive chandeliers, and lightbulbs embedded in plaster rosettes. The high-back polished wooden benches beckon you to sit, and rest rooms are available. Suburban trains arrive and leave from an attached shed; NY Waterway ferries land at the north and south sides of the main terminal. Take your time, because there are lots of details to take in.

Leaving the terminal via the cobblestone plaza, walk past the statue of Samuel Sloan, the Lackawanna president who brought the railroad into the big leagues, the brick Hoboken Land Building, and the hundred-year-old Clam Broth House to Washington Street, and turn right (north). The low-rise main street, almost entirely intact from the 1880s to 1920s, runs for 14 blocks and offers every imaginable service to the now wide diversity of residents who call Hoboken home. Once German, Italian, and Irish, the city lured Hispanics then urban professionals looking for moderately priced housing near their Lower Manhattan jobs. The best housing is now Manhattan expensive.

The stores, restaurants, and bars reflect all lifestyles but increasingly, the

Four cruise liners are seen docked at the Passenger Ship Terminal on a Sunday in July from Hamilton Park atop the Palisades in Weehawken.

trendy and upscale are taking over. On weekend evenings, Hoboken is a huge draw as a place to hang out. Restaurants and bars proliferate on Washington and the numbered cross streets, while parallel Bloomfield, Garden, and Park are residential, with some beautifully restored brownstone blocks and others reflecting the facade makeovers and aluminum awning styles of the 1950s.

Two restaurants are worth noting—Arthur's Tavern (Washington and 3rd), a steak house housed in Hoboken's oldest building that offers diners mosaic tiled floors, tin ceilings, and twenty-four- and forty-eight-ounce T-bones at bargain prices, and Helmers' (Washington and 11th), a holdover from the days when North German Lloyd and Hamburg American liners docked on the waterfront. The German beer selection is considered one of the best in the East, and the weiss wurst, schnitzel, dumplings, and red cabbage are the genuine items.

Across from Helmers', a plaque set in the median divider credits Hoboken as the site for the first games of baseball, played in nearby Elysian Fields, now reduced to tiny Elysian Park. Take 11th for 1 block west to Bloomfield and turn right at the old Columbia Club, once a German men's club and now a condominium, to sample one of the pretty residential streets. Turn right at 13th and recross Washington to the Shipyard, once the Bethlehem Steel Shipyard and now a brand-new residential complex located just to the north of the old Maxwell Coffee plant. A NY Waterway ferry landing for Manhattan leaves from alongside the marina.

Walk north along the river and turn left onto 14th. You pass storefronts that once housed one waterfront bar after another, and the former Lipton Tea plant, now an apartment complex. Using one of two suggested streets, turn right and march out of town up into the Palisades at Weehawken. For the next twenty minutes you'll be traveling on sidewalks alongside busy approaches to the Lincoln Tunnel, but there is a pot of gold at the end.

There is now only one choice for crossing the railroad tracks into Weehawken at the entrance to the Lincoln Tunnel. Cross Park Avenue, then turn right onto Willow Street and use the sidewalk on the left side. Once over the tracks, turn right at the gas station and walk 1 block to the next intersection. One road leads east to Lincoln Harbor, but you turn left along the concrete road heading north toward the Lincoln Tunnel helix. Use the right sidewalk sloping upward past a large bus parking lot (right) and the Lincoln Tunnel tollbooths (left) over the fence. The sidewalk climbs and passes under the arcing helix. Beyond the Hess station it returns to a residential neighborhood, still rising along Boulevard East. Curving up to the right, you arrive at the top of the Palisades and *voilà!* The entire island of Manhattan opens up, providing a well-deserved reward after all the shadowing traffic of the last twenty minutes.

Hamilton Park, a leafy neighborhood to the right, stretches for a couple of blocks to the south and is well worth a detour. Its promontory isolation makes it a most desirable place to live. The name refers to Alexander Hamilton, who was killed in a duel (1804) with Aaron Burr at a spot marked with a tiny memorial just to the right of where you arrived at the cliff edge.

Walk north along Boulevard East to a small park where on warm weekends the local residents gather for a chat while enjoying the million-dollar view. The park's northern end is a favorite spot for wedding pictures. Beginning at 4:30 P.M. on a Saturday or Sunday from May to October, two or more cruise ships will reverse into the Hudson from the Passenger Ship Terminal directly opposite. The ships signal their departure with backing whistles then turn and head downstream, exchanging final farewells with the docking pilot's tug.

To reach the Port Imperial ferry landing below, marked by a white ferry-boat, walk north past a World War I memorial to a stair tower of 227 steps. The hike south from the George Washington Bridge ends here, too (see Escape 17). At the bottom, Pershing Road crosses above the railroad tracks and drops down to Port Imperial, the headquarters for NY Waterway, Arthur's Landing restaurant, a marina, and a huge parking lot. The ferry operation began in 1986 initially to serve the new housing being built along the river, but the catchment area is much wider now, drawing patrons from both sides of the river.

Ferries operate every twenty minutes (every ten minutes during weekday rush hours) to West 38th Street, Manhattan, where NY Waterway's red, white, and blue ferry buses (fare included) fan out across Manhattan. At West 38th Street, bus destinations are marked in yellow on the pavement and include major crosstown streets from 57th to 34th, Lincoln Center, and downtown. It's a seamless service and very well patronized.

For More Information

NY Waterway: (800) 53–FERRY; www.nywaterway.com. There are now half a dozen NY Waterway cross-Hudson ferry landings on the New Jersey side and four on the Manhattan side. Routes are continually changing and expanding.

Hudson-Bergen Line Rail, New Jersey Transit: (973) 762–5100 or (800) 626–7433; www.njtransit.com. Now operates between two terminals in Bayonne north through Liberty State Park to Exchange Place and Newport, Jersey City, and to Hoboken.

Passenger Ship Terminal: www.nypst.com or www.worldshipny.com. Ship arrivals and departures.

Hoboken information: www.hoboken.com or www.hobokeni.com.

Arthur's Tavern: 237 Washington Street (at 3rd); (201) 656–5009.

Helmers': 1036 Washington Street (at 11th); (201) 963–3333. Closed Sunday.

17 Urban and Suburban: Hudson River and Jersey Palisades

This full-day 11-mile hike takes the George Washington Bridge to the New Jersey side of the Hudson River, then heads south through a kaleidoscope of neighborhoods at the river's edge and atop the Palisades to the Weehawken Ferry. Nearly the entire route can be duplicated by bicycle.

Itinerary at a Glance

Starting point

Outside the George Washington Bridge Bus Station, Fort Washington Avenue and West 178th Street, Manhattan.

Travel directions to starting point

Subway: Take the A train north under the Upper West Side to 175th Street, then walk north along Fort Washington Avenue to 178th Street.

Bus: From the West Side, take M5 up Sixth Avenue, Broadway, and Riverside Drive to 178th and Broadway; walk 1 block west. From the East Side, take M4 up Madison Avenue and across 110th Street then up Broadway to 178th and Fort Washington Avenue. From Harlem, take M100 west along 125th Street then north along Amsterdam Avenue and Broadway to 178th and Broadway. Walk 1 block west.

Bicycle: The best route is north from Central Park using the on-street bike lanes, first on Adam Clayton Powell Boulevard then, at 116th Street, angling left onto St. Nicholas Avenue to 168th Street. Shift to Broadway, then go 1 block west to Fort Washington Avenue.

Car: Not recommended from Manhattan, Brooklyn, or Queens.

Difficulty level and special considerations

This is a mostly flat 11-mile walk with one set of uneven stone steps down the Palisades, two relatively brief upward slopes, and one stair tower descent with 227 steps. Cyclists can avoid both sets of steps (see the itinerary).

This trek may be taken year-round, though caution is required when there is ice or snow on the stone steps between the Palisades and the river. There is no need to pack a lunch—it will be a treat to stop halfway into the hike at Mitsuwa Market Place (formerly Yaohan Plaza), the Japanese food court and supermarket in Edgewater. If you suffer from vertigo, you may want to walk along the inside rail of the pedestrian walkway over George Washington Bridge, but otherwise there should be no problems with heights. Watch out for cyclists on the bridge; while they are generally polite, this is the main route to and from New Jersey and north to Nyack.

Introduction

The New Jersey waterfront opposite the West Side of Manhattan has undergone an almost complete transformation, from industrial sites and railroad marshaling yards into a series of mostly low-rise residential riverfront complexes. The new developments share the flat platform of land between the base of the Palisades and the Hudson with existing communities that date from the turn of the twentieth century into the 1920s and 1950s. The sum total has spawned some new commercial food and clothing outlets that cater to residents and visitors.

Getting there and back is a delight. A walk or cycle across the George Washington Bridge gives outstanding long-range views to the north and south, and at a much more leisurely pace than crossing by car in heavy traffic. You have time to gaze at the majestic Palisades' natural beauty looking north to the Tappan Zee, and south to Riverside Park and the Manhattan skyline.

The chosen route allows you to sample a short portion of Palisades Interstate Park stretching north for 12 miles into New York State via the Long Path atop the Palisades and the Shore Path at river level. The amazing foresight displayed by those who in 1900 set aside this land to prevent further destruction through the stone mining has given us a natural wonder to explore in depth over many outings (see Escape 18).

The route south from the G. W. Bridge passes through all sorts of neighborhoods, working class and upscale, next to the river, inland a few blocks and

Pedestrians begin a walk across the George Washington Bridge, which links the Upper West Side of Manhattan to Fort Lee, New Jersey.

atop the Palisades, from charming single-family houses in the leafy Edgewater Colony to the high-rise apartment blocks and their million-dollar skyline views.

The return to Manhattan is via the New York Waterway Ferry owned by the Imperatore family, who spurred riverfront development by restarting a cross-Hudson service in 1986 to West 38th Street. On the Manhattan side, a dedicated ferry bus network distributes passengers to destinations between 57th Street and Lower Manhattan. A pause at Hamilton Park above the ferry landing followed by the crossing makes for a gentle way to end the day.

Itinerary

When you arrive at the starting point, the George Washington Bridge Bus Terminal is useful for the rest rooms, to buy something to drink along the way, and to pick up bus schedules for New Jersey points such as the Red and Tan Route 9A–9W for access to northern portions of Palisades Interstate Park (see Escape 18). The terminal, completed in 1963, vaguely resembles a concrete butterfly from the outside and is rather dreary and cavernous within.

From the southeast corner of Fort Washington Avenue and West 178th Street, walk or cycle 2 blocks down along West 178th Street past Pinehurst and Cabrini, noting the green-and-white bike signs that lead to a leftward-arcing concrete ramp up to the bridge's south-side foot and cycle path. Unlike the potentially lethal cyclists on the Brooklyn Bridge, most riders here give way to wayward pedestrians who are likely engrossed in the stupendous views.

A short way out onto the bridge, look straight down onto the Little Red Lighthouse that was moved here from Sandy Hook in 1921 to serve as a warning to barges and ships to stay well away from the rocky shoals of Jeffrey's Hook sticking out into the Hudson. When the George Washington Bridge was completed in 1931, the navigational lights were mounted on the bridge's underside, and the lighthouse went dark. It was relighted in 2001.

A popular children's book—*The Little Red Lighthouse and the Great Gray Bridge,* by Hildegarde Hoyt Swift and Lynd Ward—resulted in a letter-writing campaign that saved the lighthouse, and happily it become a ward of the city. Escape 1 visits the lighthouse. Part of the view below includes the Amtrak line running south along the West Side into Penn Station, and a section of Fort Washington Park as it connects to Riverbank State Park atop the North River Sanitation Plant and Riverside Park.

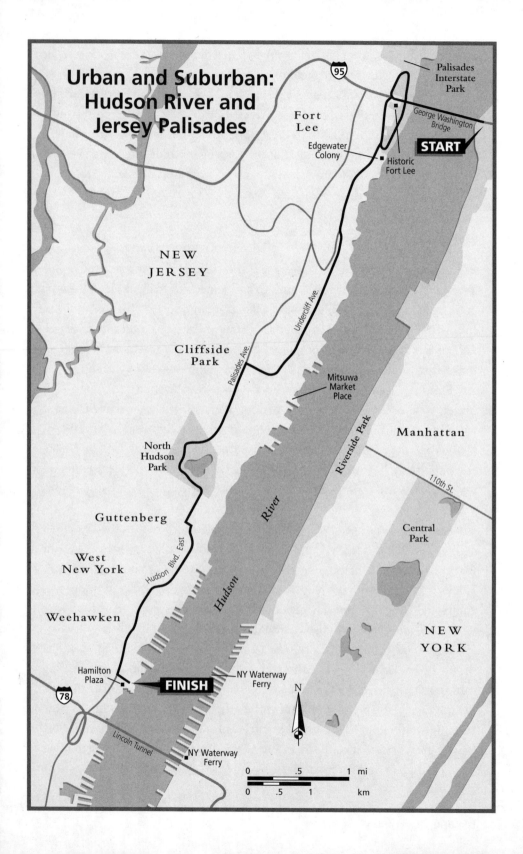

Urban and Suburban:
Hudson River and
Jersey Palisades

I-95

Fort Lee

Palisades Interstate Park

George Washington Bridge

Edgewater Colony

Historic Fort Lee

START

NEW JERSEY

Undercliff Ave.

Cliffside Park

Palisades Ave.

Mitsuwa Market Place

Manhattan

Riverside Park

North Hudson Park

110th St.

Guttenberg

Hudson River

West New York

Central Park

Hudson Blvd. East

Weehawken

NEW YORK

Hamilton Plaza

I-78

FINISH

NY Waterway Ferry

Lincoln Tunnel

N

NY Waterway Ferry

0	.5	1 mi
0	.5	1 km

On a windy day, you may feel the suspension bridge vibrate, and you will certainly be aware of the endless stream of traffic. The lower-level roadway was added in 1962, making the George Washington Bridge the world's busiest crossing, carrying some eighty-five million vehicles a year. When completed, the G. W. Bridge was the world's longest suspension span. The giant erector-set twin towers were originally designed to be encased in stone, but the depression put an end to that expense, and the result is a lighter and even more magnificent structure. The path makes a jog left around the towers.

Just to the south of the bridge on the New Jersey side sits Fort Lee, a strategic site for Revolutionary War defenses against British control of the Hudson River and New York City. In 1776, however, George Washington was forced to retreat south after Fort Washington on the Manhattan side was overtaken. Once the bridge walkway reaches terra firma in New Jersey, you can visit the site by walking south along Hudson Terrace to the entrance.

Reaching Hudson Terrace, cyclists turn left and down to River Road, where the route rejoins the hikers at the entrance to the Edgewater Colony. Hikers can do the same—but you can explore another dimension by turning right under the bridge highway approach. Just opposite a motel left across the street, a steel staircase on the right leads up into the beginning of Palisades Interstate Park. A single turquoise blue blaze indicates the beginning of the wooded Long Path north to New York State. A few minutes into the walk, you can go right to the edge of the Palisades for a look at the G. W. Bridge, Upper Manhattan, the Bronx, and up the river to Yonkers and down onto Ross Dock, a recreational area by the river.

Just a bit farther north, a double blaze and a dip in the trail indicate the beginning of the Carpenters Steps down to the river level. The 350-plus stone steps are uneven, and extra care is required if there is any ice or snow present. Keep to the path as it dives under midlevel Henry Hudson Drive to reach flat land near the river. Renovated Ross Dock has rest rooms (open during the summer season) and picnic tables.

Begin walking south to pass under the G. W. Bridge and by the small-boat landing to a scrub-fringed path bordering the river to the Edgewater Colony, a private residential community, where the path does a zigzag up the slope to the Henry Hudson Drive. Continue on the paralleling sidewalk to the busy main road coming down from Fort Lee. Here join the cyclists or shortcut hikers. The sign for the Edgewater Colony down to the left says PRIVATE, but you can make a loop through the single-family settlement along Annett Avenue

The Shore Path running below the Palisades is shown here heading south from the George Washington Bridge into the Edgewater Colony.

and back to River Road. Otherwise, cross over the road carefully and turn left onto what is now River Road, heading on the right side down the hill where soon a sidewalk begins.

Walk for about seven minutes and just before the 1908 Edgewater firehouse, turn right onto Palisade Terrace, then take the first left onto Undercliff Avenue running inland, under the cliff and still parallel to the river. This quiet street passes through a pleasant residential neighborhood, with the First Presbyterian Church coming up to the right. In about five minutes, bear right up alongside a small park, then down left as a major road sweeps down from the right to make a loop onto the continuation of Underhill. It's best to cross the road and keep right. In another five minutes, bear right, staying on Underhill where a row of houses begins.

In five minutes more, Russel Avenue leads left across River Road to Binghamton's, a floating restaurant housed aboard a 1905-built former Lackawanna Railroad ferry that took passengers and vehicles between the Hoboken Terminal and Barclay Street in Lower Manhattan. When that service ended in November 1967, the ferry was moved up here. It's worth a look to see the graceful wooden interiors and historic photo displays. At lunch or early evening, the former saloon deck offers a standard menu at reasonable prices, with great views across to the Upper West Side at the level of Riverside Church at West 120th through 122nd Streets. There is also a fancier restaurant on the former vehicle deck.

If you're not making this diversion, continue on Undercliff to Archer, turn left down to River Road, and cross to Mitsuwa Market Place, the Japanese shopping plaza, supermarket, and food court (formerly Yaohan Plaza). There

This view is across the Hudson from Edgewater, New Jersey, to Riverside Church on the Upper West Side of Manhattan.

are tables inside, usually crowded, adjacent to the appetizing food counters. Have a look around—it's a world totally different from what's outside. Shuttle buses run from here to Port Authority Bus Terminal.

After a break and a wash, return up Archer and left up Edgewater Road to the top of the Palisades. In rapid succession, walk or cycle along Cecelia to Adolphus, turn left, and pass a playground on the right. Then at George, turn left and bear right onto Laird to Palisades Avenue, which soon crosses Woodcliff into North River Park with a wooded stand and a lake. Skirt around to the right with the lake on your left, aiming for the pavilion, then cross 79th and continue straight ahead along commercial Broadway. At 74th, go left onto Hudson Boulevard, which when you have turned right becomes Boulevard East, a residential section of upscale apartments, row houses, and single-family homes.

In the next thirty minutes (walking), the boulevard passes the Galaxy Apartments, small parks overlooking Hudson opposite the 79th Street Boat Basin in Manhattan, Amvets Park, and the Cuban Memorial. At Pershing Road, cyclists and hikers, if pressed for time, can angle left and down to the

Weehawken Ferry. Otherwise, continue along the boulevard to Hamilton Plaza, a delightful neighborhood park looking over to the Passenger Ship Terminal. On weekends between May and October, cruise ships will be sailing between 4:00 and 5:00 P.M. For departure schedules, see "For More Information" below.

The park is a favorite spot for wedding photos. Along the way, you'll see the site where Aaron Burr killed Alexander Hamilton in an 1804 duel. The residential neighborhood located on a promontory overlooking the river and the Lincoln Tunnel helix is worth looping through. (Escape 16, "West of the Hudson Urban Waterfront" ends here.)

To reach the NY Waterway ferry, retrace your steps north to a metal stair tower just beyond Hamilton Plaza and descend 227 steps to Pershing Road, leading directly to the ferry terminal. The stairs may be closed in winter, necessitating a walk north to Pershing Road where it descends sharp right off the boulevard—a ten-minute detour.

The NY Waterway ferry leaves every twenty minutes on weekends. At the landing in Manhattan at West 38th Street, there are red, white, and blue ferry buses (included in the ferry fare) connecting to Midtown Manhattan between 57th and 34th Streets and to Lower Manhattan. Destinations are written in yellow paint on the pavement.

For More Information

NYC Transit Authority: (718) 330–1234; www.mta.info. Subway and bus information.

NY Waterway ferry: (800) 53–FERRY; www.nywaterway.com.

Passenger Ship Terminal: www.nypst.com or www.worldshipny.com. Passenger cruise ship schedules.

Palisades Interstate Park, New Jersey Section: (201) 768–1360; www.pipc.org/.

Mitsuwa Market Place (formerly Yaohan Plaza): River Road, Edgewater, NJ; (201) 941–8776.

18 Palisades Interstate Park, New Jersey

This 7- or 17-mile hiking route takes you across the George Washington Bridge, north atop the Palisades high above the Hudson River, then down to either the Englewood or the Alpine Boat Basin, south to the Edgewater Colony, and back up to the G. W. Bridge. Notes are included for cyclists, who take a different but parallel route.

Itinerary at a Glance

Starting point

178th Street and Fort Washington Avenue, Upper Manhattan.

Travel directions to starting point

Subway: Take the A train north to 175th Street, then walk to 178th Street.

Bus: From the West Side, take M5 north to 178th and Broadway and walk 1 block west to Fort Washington Avenue. From the East Side, take M4 north to 178th Street and Fort Washington Avenue. From Harlem, take M100 west across 125th Street and north to 178th Street and Broadway, and walk west 1 block.

Bicycle: The best route is north from Central Park using the on-street bike lanes, first on Adam Clayton Powell Boulevard then, at 116th Street, angling left onto St. Nicholas Avenue to 168th Street. Shift to Broadway, then go 1 block west to Fort Washington Avenue.

Car: There's a parking garage (fee) at the George Washington Bridge Bus Station; very limited street parking.

Difficulty level and special considerations

The hike atop the Palisades is mostly level with a few short ups and downs, and entirely flat along the river. The parallel cycle route is also largely level except at either end. The only real climbing or descending is between the two parallel paths, and both directions are moderately steep. It's an easy route to follow with an occasional surprise diversion that is carefully outlined in the itinerary. The partly wooded walk is attractive year-round apart from icy periods. Because most of the walk is near or above the river, it's a fine choice for a hot summer's day, and the fall-foliage season is a special attraction. For first-timers, it's thrilling to walk over the George Washington Bridge, and the 200-plus-foot height should present few vertigo problems, especially if you keep away from the outer railing. The Palisades' path has no precipitous drops, though some of the vista points do, and the view across to Upper Manhattan shows how wooded and dramatically elevated the northern end of the borough can be. You might be inspired to take the Manhattan-to-Bronx hike (see Escape 1). Bring a picnic lunch and water to enjoy a quiet spell along the river. Most times of year, there is at least one rest room stop, and several more in season.

Introduction

Thank the New Jersey Federation of Women's Clubs for the twin parallel paths that slice north from the George Washington Bridge into New York State. They lobbied for legislation to establish the Palisades Interstate Park Commission in 1900, thus saving a spectacular natural phenomenon from destruction through mining of the Palisades' stone and clear-cutting of trees. The rock, known as diabase (a basaltic stone) or more commonly traprock, was a popular building material for houses and roads and as ships' ballast. It is still mined farther up the Hudson; you might see traprock barges moving downriver during your hike.

The Palisades fronting on the Hudson River stretch 40 miles from Weehawken, just north of the Lincoln Tunnel helix, well into New York State at Haverstraw. The Palisades Interstate Park itself is a 2,472-acre linear greenway, often not more than 0.25 mile wide, that runs 12 miles from Fort Lee on the New Jersey side of the George Washington Bridge to the New York State line. Just 20 acres lie in New York State.

The hike or cycle ride begins for most in Upper Manhattan and includes a sensational crossing of the George Washington Bridge to begin and to end the day's outing. At Fort Lee, cyclists have access to 7-mile Henry Hudson Drive that runs first at midlevel then down to the shoreline as far north as Alpine, where the choice is a return trip or a climb up to Route 9W for an alternate way back south.

The New Jersey Palisades runs north for 12 miles from the George Washington Bridge and parallels the Hudson into New York State.

Hikers may choose the Long Path atop the Palisades for a couple of miles, then head down to the Englewood Boat Basin and take the Shore Path south; or you can opt for a longer 7-mile hike to join the path down to the Alpine Boat Basin and then south. There are excellent Hudson River viewpoints en route, some with a 330-foot sheer drop. At the south end, hikers using the Shore Path and cyclists on Henry Hudson Drive pass under the George Washington Bridge approach and swing up past Edgewater Colony, a private residential neighborhood of single-family houses, to Fort Lee, a Revolutionary War–era site, for access to the bridge path.

Itinerary

Hikers and cyclists start at the corner of 178th Street and Fort Washington Avenue in the shadow of the overpass leading into the George Washington Bridge and its bus station. The bleak terminal is useful for its public rest rooms and food and beverage outlets up one level from the street. Buses operate to New Jersey points, including Red and Tan's 9A–9W, which takes Route

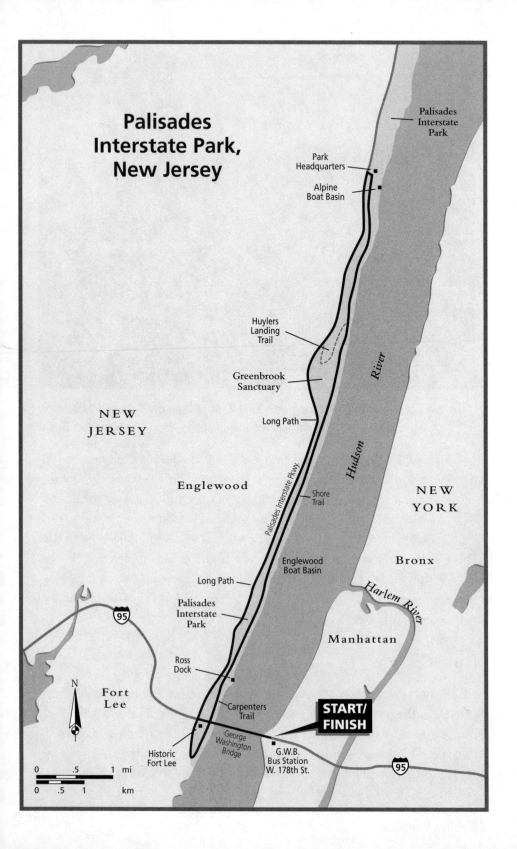

Palisades
Interstate Park,
New Jersey

Palisades
Interstate
Park

Park
Headquarters

Alpine
Boat Basin

Huylers
Landing
Trail

Greenbrook
Sanctuary

Long Path

NEW
JERSEY

Englewood

Hudson River

Palisades Interstate Pkwy.

Shore
Trail

NEW
YORK

Englewood
Boat Basin

Bronx

Long Path

Harlem River

Palisades
Interstate
Park

Manhattan

Ross
Dock

Carpenters
Trail

START/
FINISH

N

Fort
Lee

Historic
Fort Lee

George
Washington
Bridge

G.W.B.
Bus Station
W. 178th St.

0   .5   1 mi

0   .5   1   km

9W just west of the Palisades Interstate Park—a convenience for hikers who might wish to ride back into the city.

Go west along 178th Street as it descends a couple of blocks to the spiral foot and cycle path up to the south side of the G. W. Bridge. Hikers and cyclists are generally friendly to one another; two-footers have the right-of-way over two-wheelers. The bridge, completed in 1931, with its second lower deck added in 1962, is the busiest major bridge in the world, with some eighty-five million vehicles crossing annually. The engineer, Othmar H. Ammann, was also responsible for the Triboro, Bronx-Whitestone, Throgs Neck, and Verrazano-Narrows Bridges, and the bridge's architect, Cass Gilbert, had previous triumphs with the Woolworth Building and the Alexander Hamilton Custom House at Bowling Green.

The view from the bridge is directly down onto the Little Red Lighthouse, a meandering footpath that is part of a West Side hike between Riverside Park and the Bronx (see Escape 1), and the Amtrak rail line slicing through a rocky cut between Penn Station and Albany, north to Montreal, and west to Buffalo and Chicago. On a clear day, the view south extends to the skyline and to Staten Island, rising some 15 miles away. Across the bridge traffic lanes, you can see far up the Hudson to the Tappan Zee and the continuous natural beauty of the New Jersey Palisades that you will soon experience.

The bridge path zigzags around both erector-set-style towers, then lands on the Jersey side at Fort Lee, where mercifully the relentless traffic din fades away. Cyclists turn left at the first street, Hudson Terrace, which becomes River Road sloping down past the Fort Lee Historic Park; then take the first left onto Henry Hudson Drive. The road swings left below Fort Lee and above the Hudson, passes under the G. W. Bridge approach, and gradually descends to just above the river and inland from the Shore (foot) Path, first past Ross Dock, a recreation area, then Englewood Boat Basin (picnic area), Undercliff Dock (picnic area), and on past Huylers Landings. The road rises above the Alpine Boat Basin (7 miles) to Route 9W, first passing under the Palisades Interstate Parkway (PIP), completed in 1958 and running north to Bear Mountain. Cyclists are not allowed to use the PIP; instead, use parallel Route 9W.

Hikers leaving the G. W. Bridge path turn right under the bridge approach and, immediately to the right, climb the caged iron steps to the beginning of the Long Path (turquoise blue blazes) into the park. The Long Path extends well upstate to a point north of Catskill Park; long-range plans are to connect exiting sections into a greenway into the Adirondacks.

As the wooded walk continues north, several branch paths lead to the cliff edge for dramatic views of the bridge's suspension span across to Upper Manhattan and left well up the Hudson past Yonkers. Not far into the walk, the Carpenters Trail leads down some 350 often uneven stone steps to the river at Ross Dock. Continue north to the fenced-in entrance to Allison Park for comfort facilities and more great views. The Long Path shifts to the left of the drives into St. Peter's College and skirts close to the PIP. Two miles into the northward hike, a road—left to the PIP and Route 9W—also descends right with a parallel sidewalk to the Englewood Boat Basin, equipped with a comfort station, picnic tables, and refreshment stand (in season). If you're heading south, it's 3 miles back to the G. W. Bridge (see below).

Atop the Palisades, the Long Path continues north for pauses at several viewpoints. At High Tom, a deep cleft in the cliff face was used by lumberjacks to send logs down to the river. Rockefeller Lookout, shared with Palisades Interstate Parkway motorists, shows the walls and foundations of an old estate. The trail, with some up-and-down stretches, shifts inland close to the PIP while skirting the fenced-in 165-acre Greenbrook Sanctuary (accessible by appointment), a wooded wilderness of tall oaks, a five-acre pond, and a popular spot for some 250 recorded species of birds.

At the north end, a red-blazed trail leads down to Huylers Landing for the Shore Path south, now 2 miles short of Alpine Boat Basin. Alpine Lookout, the site of the former Rio Vista estate, has foundation, garden, and driveway remains. Just over a mile farther north, the Alpine Approach Trail, an old road, winds down to what was known as Closter Dock and is now the Alpine Boat Basin (comfort station and seasonal refreshment stand). A ferry ran across to Yonkers until 1954. The Blackledge-Kearny House, built over a period between the pre-Revolution and the mid–nineteenth century, tells the Palisades story as well as depicting life next to the river. The Hudson River here is home to catfish, striped bass, white perch, eels, and blue crabs. Recommended consumption is no more than once a week, but it's also much cleaner than in the recent past.

While Alpine is the suggested turnaround point, the Long Path continues a short distance to the park headquarters then on north to the New York State line. The park commission Web site offers detailed information about the route, access to the Shore Path, and bus stops for a return to the city.

The Shore Path offers an entirely different perspective from a position below the towering Palisades. It's a pretty 7-mile, water-level hike to Huylers

Landing, Englewood Boat Basin, and Ross Dock. This last area, built on a foundation of sunken barges and landfill, was recently renovated and offer good picnic and rest room facilities. Just south of Ross Dock, the path passes beneath the overhead G. W. Bridge span and a concrete small-boat landing. The path then dives into the brush between the river and the cliff, and shortly—at the perimeter of the Edgewater Colony—it loops back up the hillside to Henry Hudson Drive and ahead to the junction of River Road. Down to the left is the start of a Jersey-side 9-mile walk south to the Weehawken Ferry back to Manhattan at West 38th Street (see Escape 17).

Be very careful crossing busy River Road, but do cross it, because the west shoulder is safer for the short climb up to the path back across the George Washington Bridge, accessed just before the underpass you used to start the walk. The complete hike as far north as Englewood Boat Basin is about 7 miles, including the double bridge crossing; it's about 11 miles if you turn back at Huylers Landing, and 17 miles for the Alpine Boat Basin route.

For More Information

New York City Transit Authority: (718) 330–1234; www.mta.info. Subway and bus information.

Red and Tan Bus Lines: (212) 279–6526; www.redandtanlines.com. Route 9A–9W leaves from the Port Authority Bus Terminal to and from Alpine, Closter Dock Road, and Route 9W (forty minutes); from the George Washington Bridge Bus Station to and from Alpine, Closter Dock Road, and Route 9W (twenty minutes), for hikers who would like to return from Alpine to the city by bus.

Palisades Interstate Park Commission: Box 155, Alpine, NJ 07620; (201) 768–1360; www.pipc.org/. Excellent Web site with Palisades history, trail information, facilities, and access to Greenbrook Sanctuary.

This seaside outing begins in Spring Lake, New Jersey's Irish Riviera, and aims north along the beach and boardwalk to Victorian Ocean Grove, a bed-and-breakfast mecca—and in summer a Methodist family campground. The hike can also be done in reverse, beginning in Ocean Grove and walking south to Spring Lake. Both communities are fine places to spend one day or to extend the stay for a night or two. Swimmers must obtain beach badges in season.

Itinerary at a Glance

Starting point

Spring Lake or Ocean Grove, New Jersey.

Travel directions to starting point

Train: New Jersey Transit weekend trains leave Penn Station every two hours for Ocean Grove (use the Asbury Park station) and Spring Lake, a ride of just under two hours that becomes increasingly scenic after South Amboy (fifty minutes). Most departures require an easy cross-platform transfer at Long Branch. In summer, trains leave every hour.

Car: To reach Ocean Grove, take the New Jersey Turnpike south to Garden State Parkway exit 100B; follow Route 33E to its end and cross Route 71 into Ocean Grove. Continue along Broadway to the ocean, then head north to the gazebo at the end of Ocean Pathway, leading back to the Great Auditorium. At the end of the one-way hike, take a northbound New Jersey Transit train to Asbury Park, a ten-minute ride, and walk into Ocean Grove.

To reach Spring Lake, take the New Jersey Turnpike south to the Garden State Parkway south to exit 98. Head south on Route 34 south for 0.5 mile to a traffic circle, then turn east onto County

Route 524, Allaire Road (heading in the direction of Spring Lake). Continue east for 2.5 miles, then angle slightly right onto Warren Avenue to the North Jersey Coast Line rail crossing. Turn right and park at the station. At the end of the one-way hike, take a New Jersey Transit southbound train from Asbury Park back to Spring Lake, a ten-minute ride.

Difficulty level and special considerations

This is an easy, level 10-mile walk including suggested meanderings. This outing could be considered year-round; if you're going for a day hike, a sunny and windless out-of-season day is recommended over a hot shadeless July or August day. For overnighters, bed-and-breakfast inns will consider a one-night stay rather than two over a nonholiday off-season weekend, so you can start out on a Saturday morning, stay over, then have all day Sunday before returning home. Because maritime climates are notoriously fickle, any forecast of rain, especially if combined with wind, begs foul-weather gear. There is precious little shelter between end points.

Introduction

Seaside New Jersey offers an amazingly varied string of locales that serve equally well for a day at the beach or a short-stay bed-and-breakfast destination, and as a suburban bedroom community. The so-named North Jersey Coast begins at Sandy Hook and continues south through Long Branch and Asbury Park to Bay Head, the south end of the New Jersey Transit line from Manhattan.

The most distinctive towns with lots to offer the hiker and sight-seer are Spring Lake and Ocean Grove, separated by a nearly continuous seaside promenade of 7 miles. On a full-day outing, both towns are worth at least two hours each to explore, more to have a meal; the two are also popular as a weekend outing to range even farther.

Spring Lake is the leafiest of all the communities, and the town has strict regulations to keep it first and foremost a pleasant place to live. That means not encouraging raucous day-trippers with the clutter of boardwalk attractions and fast-food outlets found in some adjacent towns. Architecturally, the town is a treasure trove of seaside and suburban residential architecture, ranging from high Victorian to screened-in porch clapboard and trophy-house Mediterranean. Third Avenue, the main street, is low-key and equally useful for the visitor and resident, with decent delis and lunch restaurants and

The Boardwalk at Spring Lake, New Jersey, runs north along the Atlantic beaches to Belmar, Avon-by-the-Sea, Bradley Beach, Ocean Grove, and Asbury Park.

attractive book, clothing, crafts, and collectibles shops.

As you leave town by the north gate, Asbury Park's skyline looms some 7 miles ahead. The seaside walk is part boardwalk, part concrete promenade, and part sidewalk. In the off-season, when beach badges (a fee) are not required, you can also drop down to the sand and continue north. The communities through which you pass are mostly typical seaside clutter, but you will find attractive residential neighborhoods if you are willing to dive inland a few blocks. Still, most folks will want to stick to the straight and narrow and treat this section as a brisk sea-air hike to Ocean Grove—a really special destination.

Ocean Grove was built as a Methodist summer tented campground in the second half of the nineteenth century, and that traditional function is very much alive clustered around the wooden Great Auditorium. Subsequent prosperity and changing lifestyles have produced a dense collection of colorful wooden Victorian row houses both large and small. Today they are occupied as year-round residences, and used as summer homes and bed-and-breakfast inns. Some of the strict Methodist rules still exist, so you won't find a singles bar scene, and you cannot go to the beach until after 12:30 P.M. on Sunday. But the town has many fine places to stay and excellent restaurants.

My wife and I have stayed as paying guests at four of the bed-and-breakfast places mentioned in the text (two in Spring Lake and two in Ocean Grove), and we have paid for our meals at the restaurants and cafes listed. Both towns have excellent Web sites; have a look for additional suggestions.

Itinerary

Getting there by car is routine turnpike and parkway driving, but those taking the New Jersey Transit train are rewarded with a scenic approach to the coast. Be sure to take a seat on the left-hand side leaving Penn Station. Leaving the high-speed Northeast Corridor Line at Rahway, the train shifts to the North Jersey Coast branch and, after the Perth Amboy stop, crosses the mouth of the Raritan River. Views of Raritan Bay, Lower New York Bay, and tidal marshes open up. On a clear day, you can look straight north across the water to the Verrazano-Narrows Bridge (14 miles).

Note the pretty gingerbread Victorian Red Bank station (left) and the stone and peaked-roof version at Little Silver (left) and Monmouth Park racetrack (right). After several river crossings, overhead electrification ends at Long Branch, and you change to the diesel-powered Bay Head shuttle across the platform. From here, the train blows at every crossing, and by looking down the streets to the left you can get glimpses of the ocean.

If you're walking from or staying in Ocean Grove, get off at Asbury Park and walk to Ocean Grove by heading right from the station along Main Street. Once you're across the short bridge, go left into Ocean Grove toward the Great Auditorium and the ocean. If you're getting off at Spring Lake, its pretty station is now a bank where the sign above one door reads WAITING ROOM and another MONEY.

Spring Lake developed as a serious resort in 1875 after the Central of New Jersey railway arrived. By the turn of the century, it boasted numerous large seaside hotels, a couple of which remain standing today. Sadly, the venerable Warren, built between 1874 and 1890, was demolished in 2000. The hulking Essex and Sussex (1914) at the bottom end of the lake remains, however, and has reopened as a condominium for mature adult residents. Gradually, the prosperous community developed into a bedroom suburb. Because the majority of its population was and is Irish American, Spring Lake took on the title of the Irish Riviera. Apart from a few tracts where hotels used to stand and

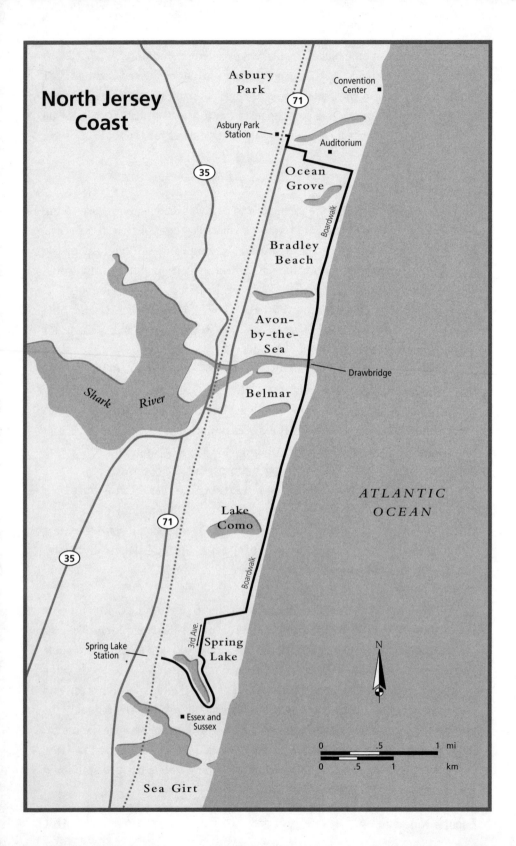

North Jersey Coast

Asbury Park

Convention Center

71

Asbury Park Station

Auditorium

Ocean Grove

35

Boardwalk

Bradley Beach

Avon-by-the-Sea

Drawbridge

Shark River

Belmar

ATLANTIC OCEAN

Lake Como

71

Boardwalk

35

3rd Ave.

Spring Lake Station

Spring Lake

N

Essex and Sussex

0   .5   1   mi

0   .5   1   km

Sea Girt

some trophy houses replacing more modest dwellings, the place has changed very little since the 1920s. Because of its residential nature, Spring Lake changes very little between seasons, though the height of summer will see an influx of family day-trippers who head mostly to the beach.

From the station platform, walk back to the level crossing and turn right into town. A small block of shops to the left lines Warren Avenue. At the end, the Chateau, an inn, faces the park in which sits the serpentine Spring Lake. Follow the path with the lake to your left to St. Catherine's Roman Catholic Church, where if it's a Saturday there's likely to be a wedding, and on Sunday several masses. At other times, have a look inside to see the opulent interiors, gilt capitals, dome, coffered arched ceiling, religious paintings, and stained glass. The church was built to resemble a scaled-down St. Peter's Basilica in Rome.

The few remaining summer hotels are just off to the right as you follow the serpentine around the backside of the yellow Essex and Sussex. Skip the beach for now and continue along First Avenue, the start of a beautiful residential neighborhood that stretches north for 15 blocks and inland for several blocks. Ashling Cottage, facing the lake, is one fine place to stay. Passaic and Third mark the south end of the main shopping street, which runs for 5 blocks. Stop here to have a bite or buy supplies for a picnic to be enjoyed later during the walk. More residential streets cross to the left and right. Zigzag to your heart's content.

Following Third to Tuttle, turn right for an attractive street of substantial houses and several B&Bs, including the Italianate-style Normandy Inn built in 1888. All welcome callers, and if this is your first visit to Spring Lake, check them out as you pass and take a brochure for a possible weekend.

Now it's time to head to the boardwalk, one that was substantially rebuilt following the winter storm of 1992 that destroyed entire sections all the way to Asbury Park and took away much of the beach. Every community has responded differently to the damage; Spring Lake, being very well off, has done more restoration that others to the north. The materials used are more durable and less likely to splinter than wood.

Tuttle leads to the beachfront, and opposite, the North End Beach Pavilion sells beach badges and has a snack bar and changing room. Be sure to have a look at the terra-cotta bas-reliefs of fish, seashells, and lighthouses embedded in the walls. The boardwalk runs south for 2 miles to Sea Girt, an equally quiet place, but the main event aims north. From the pavilion, the 7-mile walk passes through the north end gate (Lake Como is to the left) and on past

Belmar, across the Shark River Inlet via a drawbridge into Avon-by-the-Sea. There is usually considerable fishing boat activity along the waterway. Just inland on the Belmar side, several seafood restaurants cluster by the first road bridge. The boardwalk, because of the 1992 storm, is intermittent, but there is a continuous walkway on through Bradley Beach to Ocean Grove, with its distinctive Victorian style, the line of demarcation.

Sandwiched between not-so-quaint Bradley Beach, the ocean, the railroad tracks, and the wreck of what once was the major resort of Asbury Park, it is amazing that Ocean Grove is still intact. In fact, before it became a National Historic District, many of its wooden Victorians were in disrepair. Rescued by people looking for affordable housing and others interested in restoration, Ocean Grove is again prosperous and preserved in a very real way.

Established by the Ocean Grove Camp Meeting Association in 1869, it became a Methodist tented summer community much like Sea Cliff on Long Island and Oak Bluffs on Martha's Vineyard. Gradually, shacks were added to the tents that sat on wooden platforms; then true Victorian houses sprouted, some quite substantial, resulting in today's vast collection, one of the largest in America. Once there were 1,000 tents; today 114 platform tents are attached to little bungalows sited around the Great Auditorium. Some rent for the entire summer by the same families each year, and others for shorter periods.

The Great Auditorium, a huge wooden structure built in 1894 with 6,500 theater-style seats, faces a grassy mall that leads down to the Memorial Pavilion, boardwalk, and beach. Today it's used by the Camp Meeting Association for religious services, family gatherings, and all sorts of musical programs, from organ recitals to classical concerts, John Philip Sousa's music, singing groups, soloists, Broadway musicals, and more.

The Camp Meeting Association still owns the land, but municipal power comes from Neptune Township. Once the rules were no fishing, swimming, sunbathing, or even hanging out the wash. No automobiles were allowed on Sunday until 1977, when the *New York Daily News* broke the ban by saying freedom of speech allowed newspaper delivery. Still, the beach does not open on Sunday until after church at 12:30; there are no bars; and residents are not allowed to consume alcohol on the front porch.

Some notable buildings surrounding the Great Auditorium are Beersheba Well (1870), Centennial Cottage (1874), Bishop Janes Tabernacle (1877), and Thornley Chapel (1889).

Main Avenue, 5 blocks north of Broadway, the first major street that runs

Here's a row of Victorian cottages along the Ocean Pathway in Ocean Grove, New Jersey.

left when you enter Ocean Grove proper, has the village shops and a few very good restaurants such as Captain Jack's and a lively place for lunch, Nagles Apothecary Café. Eight more blocks running inland from the sea are worth exploring, and the town has a long roster of bed-and-breakfast inns, some of which you might wish to inspect. We have stayed at Ocean Plaza, facing the Ocean Pathway, and at Carol Inn, on Pitman, near the boardwalk 2 blocks north of Main Avenue. While it's busy here in summer—but never rowdy—an off-season weekend is a truly tranquil getaway with the sea at your doorstep and excellent restaurants to finish off the day.

The hulking structures looming just to the north in Asbury Park are the Convention Center, Casino, and the Berkeley Cartaret Hotel, faded remnants of what was the largest resort north of Atlantic City. The adventurous might want to explore the boardwalk relics, but otherwise there is little to see except dilapidation and empty lots. The sharp contrast across Wesley Lake between Ocean Grove and Asbury Park is a bit overwhelming to fathom.

When you are ready to leave Ocean Grove, walk right around the Great Auditorium and through the tented campground, angling farther to the right to cross Wesley Lake by one of the short bridges. Continue a few blocks through Asbury Park's business district to north–south Main Street, paralleling the railroad tracks. The station building is obvious, and the waiting room will be closed on weekends. No doubt, if you came by train, you will have purchased a round-trip excursion fare. The train whistles its way up from the south, and again, you change at Long Branch for Penn Station. Motorists can buy a one-way ticket from a machine on the platform for the ten-minute, three-stop ride back to their cars at Spring Lake. If the vending machines are working, there is a $3.00 penalty if you buy a ticket from the train conductor.

For More Information

New Jersey Transit: (973) 762–5100; in New Jersey only, (800) 772–2222; www.nytransit.com.

Spring Lake Chamber of Commerce: P.O. Box 694, Spring Lake, NJ 07762; (732) 449–0577; www.springlake.org.

Ashling Cottage: 106 Sussex Avenue; (732) 449–3553 or (888) 274–5464; www.Ashlingcottage.com.

Normandy Inn: 21 Tuttle Avenue; (732) 449–7172 or (800) 449–1888; www.normandyinn.com.

Sandpiper Inn: 7 Atlantic Avenue; (732) 449–6060 or (800) 824–2779. Dining.

Spring Lake Pizzeria: 1110 Third Avenue; (732) 449–9595. Italian menu.

Ocean Grove Chamber of Commerce: P.O. Box 415, Ocean Grove, NJ 07756; (732) 774–1391; www.oceangrovenj.com/.

Ocean Grove Camp Meeting Association: www.oceangrove.org/ or, for links to several related sites, www.oceangrove.org/links.htm.

Carol Inn B&B: 11 Pitman Avenue, Ocean Grove, NJ 07756; (732) 502–0303; fax (732) 776–6174.

Ocean Plaza Hotel: 18 Ocean Pathway, Ocean Grove, NJ 07756; (732) 774–6552 or (888) 891–9442; www.ogplaza.com/seeyou.htm.

Captain Jack's: 68 Main Street; (732) 869–0770. Run by the owners of Ocean Plaza.

Nagles Apothecary Café: 43 Main Street; (732) 776–9797.

Hagstrom Map of Monmouth County: Hagstrom Map and Travel Center, 57 West 43rd Street, New York, NY 10036; (212) 398–1222.

20 Delaware & Raritan Canal

There are two excursions described in this escape. First is an 8-mile hike mostly along a leafy canal towpath from Bound Brook to New Brunswick, New Jersey. And there's a 20-mile hiking and cycling wooded route parallel to the historic Delaware & Raritan Canal from Bound Brook to Princeton, New Jersey.

Itinerary at a Glance

Starting point

Penn Station, Manhattan.

Travel directions to starting point

Subway: A, C, and E trains to Penn Station, 34th Street, and Eighth Avenue; #1, #2, and #3 trains to Penn Station, 34th Street, and Seventh Avenue.

Bus: M20 up Eighth Avenue; M10 and M20 down Seventh Avenue; M16 and M34 across 34th Street; M4 and Q32 (from Queens) down Fifth Avenue, then west on 34th to Seventh Avenue and 32nd Street.

Car: Because the canal hike is one-way in rural areas, there is no public transportation back to the starting point.

Difficulty level and special considerations

Both hikes are completely level and mostly on gravel and dirt surfaces. For cyclists, the routes can be muddy after rain, and the shorter route to New Brunswick is less attractive than the much longer one to Princeton. The 20-mile hike from Bound Brook to Princeton is the longest in the book; if you conk out, there is one escape point at Kingston, cutting off the last 4 miles, for a bus back to Port Authority Bus Terminal. Because of the largely rural nature of both these routes—one of their great attractions—there are few places to buy food. Bring along your own supplies, including water, for a shady picnic.

Introduction

The Delaware & Raritan Canal predated the railroads, and from the day it opened in June 1834 it became the main route between New York and Philadelphia (at that time the Atlantic Ocean passage was considered dangerous and circuitous). Passenger service was short lived because of competing railroads, but cargo barges carrying coal (80 percent of the tonnage), bricks, stone, cement, soda ash, oil, lumber, grain, and farm produce lasted into the twentieth century. In the peak years, 1866–1871, more freight was carried by the D&R than by any other U.S. canal. The canal remained profitable until 1892; its last full year of operation was 1931. By then the mighty Pennsylvania Railroad, which had controlled it for years, put it out of business.

The 44-mile-long canal ran from New Brunswick, at the headwaters of navigation of the Raritan River, to Bordentown, the head of navigation on the Delaware, just below Trenton. A 22-mile feeder canal ran along the Delaware River from Frenchtown to Trenton to provide a steady supply of water. Fourteen wooden locks (oak and cypress) were built to carry the canal to its mighty summit—57 feet—near Trenton, with seven locks on either side of the state capital. Locks' length was enlarged from 110 feet to a very generous 220 feet, and the regulation depth was 8 feet. There were no height restrictions until 1903, so there was no need to load or unload barges at either end, reducing transfer costs between New York and Camden/Philadelphia. The main and feeder canals created towns such as South Bound Brook, East Millstone, New Hope, and Lambertville, and many important industries established themselves near the water supply. Mules pulled barges along the towpath right up to the end, but after the 1840s, steam tugs did more and more of the work.

The D&R appeared on the National Register of Historic Places in 1973, and in 1974 New Jersey designated the entire system a state park. The canal near Trenton was filled in to create a new Route 1, and a short piece was lost under Route 18 at New Brunswick, but otherwise it remains an almost continuous waterway for its entire length: 36 miles of the main canal and 22 miles of the feeder canal. The linear park is 70 miles, and the canal and towpath are part of the National Recreational Trail System. Boating, paddle and electric motors only, is a very popular pastime.

Sights to see while using the main canal route include attractive stone villages in a still-isolated section of New Jersey, nineteenth-century bridges, locks, bridgetenders' houses, spillways, and stone-arched culverts. Canoes are available for rent at Griggstown and Princeton. Trout are stocked in the Princeton section; year-round species include largemouth bass, bluegill, catfish, perch, and pickerel.

Itinerary

New Jersey Transit operates train service between Penn Station and Bound Brook, with a change of train at Newark, Penn Station. Board a Northeast Corridor or North Jersey Coast Line train at Penn for the fifteen-minute ride to Newark. Change platforms for the diesel-hauled Raritan Valley Line train to Bound Brook, the eighth stop and an hour's semiscenic two-train ride from New York. Hikers bound for the shorter route to New Brunswick will return on an hourly New Jersey Transit train from there, a direct trip of just under an hour. The longer outing to Princeton will return via the hourly New Jersey Transit shuttle to Princeton Junction, then the Northeast Corridor train back to Penn Station, New York, a trip of one hour, forty minutes. Cyclists may wish to ride directly to Princeton Junction.

Bound Brook (where you get off) and South Bound Brook across the Raritan River certainly give evidence of the word *junction,* with two rail lines coming together and then dividing, the Delaware & Raritan Canal, and several intersecting roads. From the attractive rail station, now a restaurant, you might consider a brief walk into Bound Brook's nearby residential section: Take Mountain Avenue leading north away from Main Street (left from the station) 3 blocks to Franklin Avenue, turn right, then go 2 blocks to East Street and turn right again. You pass a small park commemorating the Revolutionary War's April 13, 1777, Battle of Bound Brook, one of a string of Washington's battles that began at Trenton and Princeton.

To reach the towpath from the station, turn right along Main Street parallel to the tracks, then right on South Main under the Raritan Valley Line and up across the active CSX freight rail line. The Delaware & Raritan Canal towpath is located between the canal and the Raritan River. To the right it's 20 miles to Princeton; to the left it's 8 miles to New Brunswick.

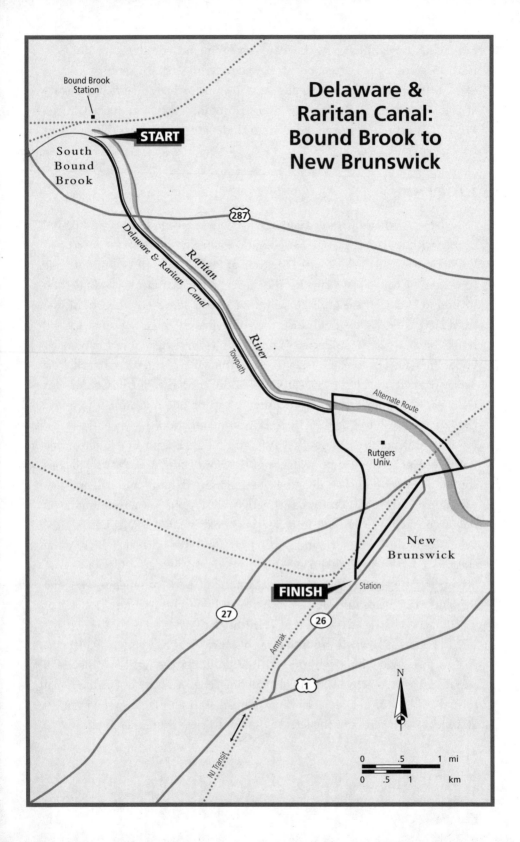

Option 1: Bound Brook to New Brunswick

The towpath parallels the canal and varies its distance from the attractive Raritan River from being adjacent to it to well out of sight, somewhat depending on the foliage season. The route is easy to follow, and there are a few diversions to take, none very far. The path shortly crosses an abandoned rail line. The first lock, dam, and guard gate are reached after the 7/37 marker, indicating distances to either end of the canal. The first number decreases in this direction, and the second increases. Right through the trees, you will see the looming Ukrainian Orthodox Church of the U.S.A. and St. Andrews Memorial Church, Seminary, Cemetery and Cultural Center. A spillway crosses the path, taking water from the canal to the river. Then a lock, canal house, and footbridge appear, making an attractive historic collection. Almost immediately, the path passes under I–287 and continues on a raised embankment between the Raritan River on the left and the D&R canal.

Shortly after marker 3/41 and a swing bridge over the Raritan River (now fixed), the towpath abruptly ends at a major spillway, with the city of New Brunswick directly ahead. Because of Route 18, you can go no farther, so turn around and walk back to the bridge. You now have a choice of a direct thirty-minute route into New Brunswick through a small park, a residential area, and a portion of the Rutgers University campus; or a longer fifty-minute trek across the river and into an attractive park leading to the next bridge back over the Raritan River into New Brunswick.

To follow the first, shorter option, face Bound Brook (the way you came) turn left over the canal and at the intersection cross over George Street and climb up into the parking lot of a high-rise apartment complex. Follow the lot, running parallel to George Street (just below) and the apartments (to your right), then cross a small street into leafy Buccleuch Park. Continue upward in the same direction to a path heading slightly left down into a ravine and up past a shelter, then flat across a playing field to the Wyckoff Street entrance. Proceed ahead through a moderately attractive working class neighborhood. After about six blocks, Wyckoff runs into Easton Avenue, leading into New Brunswick city center and the looming elevated railroad line ahead. The former Pennsylvania Railroad main line, now Amtrak owned, is the busiest and fastest passenger track in the country. New Jersey Transit trains back to New York leave from the platform on the far side.

For the longer return trip, turn right over the fixed swing bridge and cross

A wooden bridge helps hikers and cyclists to cross a spillway on the Delaware and Raritan Canal towpath from Bound Brook to New Brunswick, New Jersey.

the river to Johnson Park, a Middlesex County–maintained facility that runs for 2 miles along the Raritan River's north side. There are curving paved paths, rest rooms, and picnic tables set out under the trees. At the far end, the park ends at the stone-arched railroad bridge, which, when completed in 1903, became the first fixed structure to limit the height of the canal traffic, to 50 feet. Use River Road to cross under the arched bridge and reach Raritan Avenue, where the highway bridge will take you back across the river and into New Brunswick proper. It's now a ten- to fifteen-minute walk up to the station; the New Jersey Transit train for New York leaves from this side.

Option 2: Bound Brook to Princeton

For the much longer hike and cycle route, leave Bound Brook via South Main Street under the Raritan Valley Line and across the active CSX freight line. At the towpath, turn right for Princeton. The first marker says 8/35 (8 miles to New Brunswick, and 35 to the canal's end at the Delaware River). The last marker will be 27/17, so by putting together the short bit from the Bound Brook station and

Here the towpath passes a lock along the Delaware and Raritan Canal between Bound Brook and Princeton, New Jersey, a 20-mile hike.

nearly 2 miles to the Princeton station, the trip adds up to 20 miles.

The towpath is located on the north side of the canal, with the Raritan River on the right. You pass a spillway, then go under the I–287 overpass. In another fifteen minutes, there's a footbridge at the junction of the Raritan and Millstone Rivers, the latter of which the canal and towpath now follow. There is a locktender's house here. At 11/33, the attractive campus buildings of Alma T. White College are off to the right, a Christian center for more than one hundred years with a powerful FM transmitter. You now enter one of the most rural sections of the Garden State; active farmland fringes the route. A former canal house is located next to the Manville Causeway, which leads right and over the Millstone River into Manville Boro.

Just after 13/31, the path enters Colonial Park. Ten minutes later, Amwell Road leads left into East Millstone, a creation of the canal, and Millstone right across the river, settled earlier by the Dutch in 1690. Both are attractive small communities and sell food and beverages. In about forty minutes, you'll arrive at Blackwells Mills, one of the most picturesque points on the entire towpath

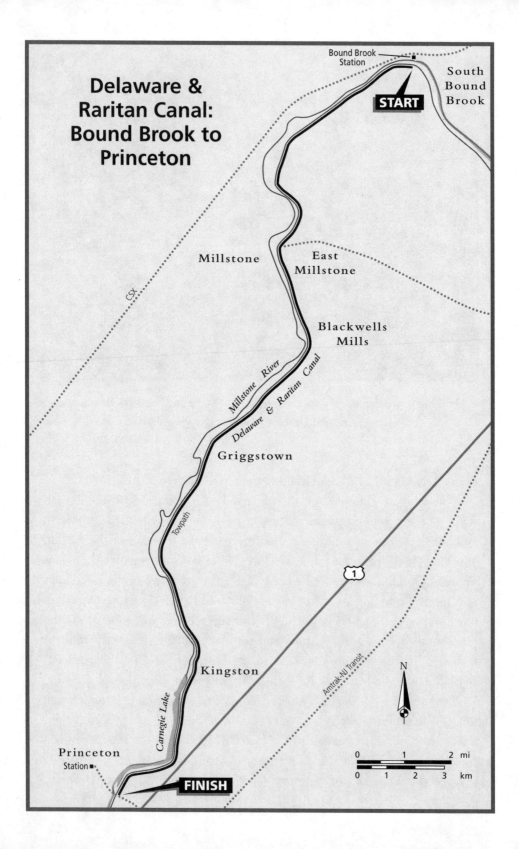

Delaware &
Raritan Canal:
Bound Brook to
Princeton

Bound Brook
Station

START

South
Bound
Brook

Millstone

East
Millstone

Blackwells
Mills

CSX

Millstone River

Delaware & Raritan Canal

Griggstown

Towpath

1

Kingston

Carnegie Lake

Amtrak-NJ Transit

N

Princeton
Station

FINISH

0   1   2 mi

0   1   2   3 km

with a fine collection of structures. A mill and a bridge across the Millstone River existed here from the 1740s; the place later became a canal loading point for agricultural products. A canal house (1835) and the park's headquarters are located here.

It's a wooded tranquil hour's walk to Griggstown, another early Dutch farm settlement, followed by a mid-eighteenth century gristmill, a wooden bridge, a bridgetender's house, and the muletender's barracks, making a most attractive little community. A causeway crosses the river here to a shady park where there are picnic tables and toilets. You can also rent canoes and kayaks for a paddle on this stretch of canal.

In less than an hour, you pass midway canal marker 22/22, and forty-five minutes later arrive at Kingston, established early as an important way stop between New York and Philadelphia. (Kingston is the only place on the hike that has bus service back to New York. From the towpath, walk up the main road into town for the bus stop—see below.) The Lincoln Highway crosses here, and a mill, bridge, locks, and lock buildings recall the canal era. In 1906, the damming of Stony Brook and the Millstone created Lake Carnegie, along which the towpath and canal follow south into Princeton.

After a bend to the right, the canal crosses the Millstone on an impressive stone aqueduct, and the path continues beyond Harrison Street to Washington Road. Left takes cyclists to Princeton Junction (a longish walk this late in the day); right crosses Lake Carnegie to the Princeton University campus.

Princeton is a daylong destination in itself, but briefly, Washington Road leads uphill between playing fields and Palmer Stadium to the main campus. A mile from the canal, you reach Nassau Street, the town's main commercial artery. For the shortest route to the Princeton rail station, go left at the topmost playing fields and cut across the campus, Elm Drive, then turn right just after the tennis courts. The station is to the left opposite McCarter Theater. The "dinky" will include a single coach; at the junction, cross under the line for trains to New York. Suburban Transit buses operate from Palmer Square to Port Authority (one hour, forty-five minutes).

For More Information

New Jersey Transit: (973) 762–5100 (from New York City and outside New Jersey); (800) 772–2222 (in New Jersey); www.njtransit.com.

Suburban Transit Co.: (800) 222–0492; www.suburbantransit.com. Hourly buses on Sunday, more frequent on Saturday, from Kingston, New Jersey, to Port Authority (one hour, forty minutes) or to Princeton–Palmer Square (ten minutes).

Delaware & Raritan Canal State Park: 625 Canal Road, Somerset, NJ 08873; (732) 873–3050; www.dandrcanal.com.

Griggstown Canoe and Kayak Rental: (908) 359–5970.

Hudson River Rail Guide

This appendix accompanies:

Escape 12, Old Croton Aqueduct Trailway

Escape 13, Bear Mountain

Escape 14, The Hudson Highlands

Escape 15, Mount Beacon

Metro-North Railroad's 74-mile Hudson Line from Grand Central to Pough-keepsie provides one of the finest scenic rides in the country and gives direct access to hiking trails, cycling routes, and historic properties from a dozen stations. You get superb water-level views of the Hudson Valley, the towering New Jersey Palisades, the rugged Hudson Highlands, sprawling country estates, the mighty fortress at West Point, and parallel river traffic. Use this appendix when taking the above outings, even when you're using the car, because to avoid backtracking, you will be taking the train to or from the hike. "Hudson River Valley" in Appendix B offers a list of significant destinations for additional day trips.

Metro-North trains depart from Grand Central Terminal at 42nd Street and Park Avenue. Purchase tickets before boarding to avoid paying a $2.00 penalty to the conductor. The ticket window line wait rarely exceeds ten minutes; it's often less. On weekends and weekdays outside rush hour, off-peak one-way fares are in effect. Grand Central Terminal offers oodles of food and beverage outlets, so consider assembling a picnic before taking the train. When buying tickets at stations other than Grand Central, use the ticket machines or buy them from the conductor (no penalty) when the station ticket offices are closed, which is generally the case on weekends. The exceptions are Croton-Harmon and Poughkeepsie.

On weekdays, weekends, and holidays, two basic services operate, each one hourly. The local trains to Croton-Harmon (33 miles) make all stops and take just over an hour to cover the complete run. The express trains to Poughkeepsie (74 miles) make limited stops—Marble Hill (connection with West Side Broadway subway #1), Yonkers, Tarrytown, Ossining, Croton-Harmon—then all stops to Poughkeespie. It takes about eighty minutes to reach Cold Spring (for the Hudson Highlands) and just under two hours to reach the end of Metro-North service. Two stations specifically designed for hikers and cyclists—Manitou and Breakneck—are served on weekends only by two morning trains up and two afternoon trains back. Weekends schedules have different patterns at rush hour, and no Monday-through-Friday trains stop at either Manitou or Breakneck.

When leaving Grand Central, choose a seat on the left-hand side. On busy weekends, it's best to board the train at least twenty minutes before departure to secure a riverside view.

The Hudson River rail line extends about 140 miles from Manhattan to Albany, and the tracks are shared by Metro-North and Amtrak trains. Metro-North serves twenty-seven stations from Grand Central to Poughkeepsie, while Amtrak trains departing from Penn Station serve stops north of Poughkeepsie—Rhinecliff, Hudson, and Albany-Rensselaer.

The Hudson River Railroad passenger service between Chambers Street in Manhattan and Poughkeepsie began in 1849; in 1871, a connection was completed at Spuyten Duyvil in the Bronx to bring the trains along the Harlem River into several Grand Central Terminals, sited at different locations over the years until the present Beaux Arts building was completed in 1913. Accompanying the new all-electric New York Central Railroad terminal was the covering of the tracks along Park Avenue from 42nd to 97th Street, and third-rail electrification to Croton-Harmon. Today's locomotives have a switch to change between electric and diesel power.

Upon leaving Grand Central, darkness prevails for about ten minutes, until at 97th Street the line pops into daylight in Harlem and runs over a stone viaduct down the middle of Park Avenue. Harlem's main street, 125th Street, is the first station stop—and a beautifully restored one, though the immediate neighborhood is shabby but improving. Shortly, the train crosses the Harlem River and swings left into the South Bronx, separating from Metro-North's Harlem and New Haven Lines, and is soon paralleling the Harlem River. Before the train passes under the arched bridge carrying the 1842-built Croton Aqueduct, look left up to the graceful stone Highbridge Water Tower, completed in 1872 to equalize the aqueduct's water pressure.

The Metro-North Hudson Line offers both a scenic train ride and access to the Old Croton Aqueduct Trailway, Bear Mountain, the Hudson Highlands, and Mount Beacon.

The Old Croton Aqueduct provides a 30-mile walk (see Escape 12) and is easily accessed from numerous Hudson Line stations.

The line swings left to pass through Marble Hill and Spuyten Duyvil, two Bronx stations across the Harlem River from Manhattan's very northern tip. The hike up the West Side (Escape 1) crosses here at right angles, from wooded Inwood Hill Park (seen rising to the left) into the Bronx using the Henry Hudson Bridge, under which the train now passes.

Ahead, the swing bridge spanning the Harlem River entrance carries Amtrak trains from Penn Station up the West Side to merge with the Metro-North Hudson Line as it now veers sharply right to parallel the Hudson River. Look south to the George Washington Bridge and across the river to Palisades Interstate Park (see Escape 17). The four-track main line is now truly a water-level route just a few feet in from the river. The express and local trains stop at Yonkers (Old Croton Trailway, Escape 12), with the city's recreation pier seen to the left and the former Otis Elevator plant to the right.

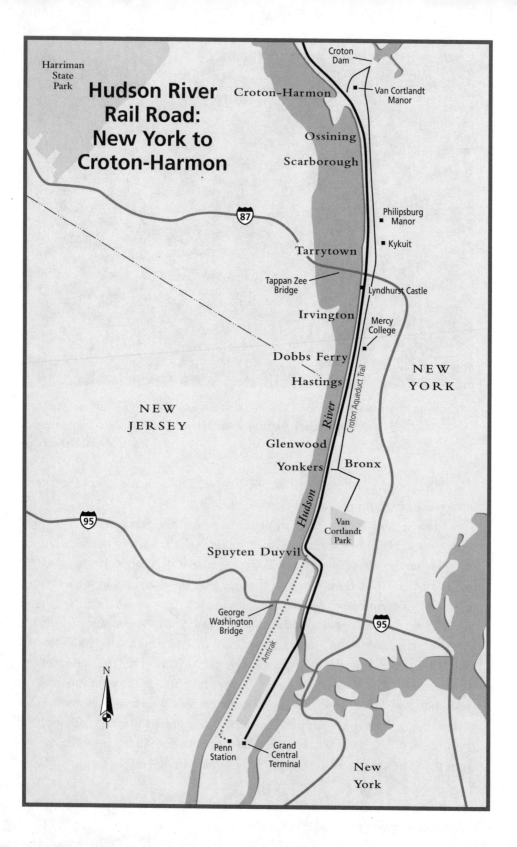

Fishermen will be out in force on weekends, and it is again safe to eat the catch, though everyday consumption is not recommended. Note the attractive stone station at Dobbs Ferry before the line begins to skirt the Tappan Zee, the Hudson's widest point. New York State replaces New Jersey along the western shore. Irvington is the location of Washington Irvington's Historic Hudson Valley house at Sunnyside and Victorian Gothic Lyndhurst Castle, owned by the National Trust for Historic Preservation (see Escape 12). Just before the stop at Tarrytown, the train passes under the Tappan Zee Bridge carrying the New York State Thruway north to Albany and west to Buffalo.

The next local stop is Philipse Manor, for Philipsburg Manor, a former seventeenth-century Dutch farming complex operated by Historic Hudson Valley. From the train, there is a long-range view north to the Hudson Highlands; Scarborough, a local stop, gives access to the aqueduct trailway (see Escape 12). Just before Ossining, an express and local stop, the stone walls of Sing Sing Prison parallel the tracks.

Slowing down, the train enters the Croton-Harmon railyards, Metro-North's maintenance facility. In the days of steam, the New York Central trains changed engines here. Now the locomotives have a switch that allows them to operate with third-rail electrification and diesel power, the latter mode now taking over. Croton-Harmon is the stop for Van Cortlandt Manor, another Historic Hudson Valley property and the northern access from the Old Croton Trailway.

The train will now begin whistling for level crossings. At Peekskill, the line arcs west toward Bear Mountain State Park and the Bear Mountain Bridge. A flag rises above the trees marking the Bear Mountain Inn. (See Escape 13 for the Bear Mountain hike.) The river becomes noticeably narrower, and rocky outcroppings briefly cut off the river view. It is here that Hudson Highlands cross, and the channel under the Bear Mountain Bridge (suspension) dramatically deepens to more than 300 feet as the surrounding land rises steeply.

Two morning weekend trains stop at Manitou for access to Bear Mountain and the Appalachian Trail coming down from New England, passing over the Bear Mountain Bridge, then continuing southwest through the Middle Atlantic states to Georgia. On the clifftops opposite, the grounds of the U.S. Military Academy at West Point begin, marked first by officers' houses, the Hotel Thayer, and then the gray-stone fortress-style buildings. At the base of the cliff, a launch docked near the West Shore Line station brings cadets and officers across the Hudson to the Garrison station for trains to New York. The

A northbound Metro-North Hudson Line train stops twice a day on weekends only at Breakneck's short platform to serve hikers bound for the Hudson Highlands.

colorful cluster of wooden Victorian buildings across the street from the Garrison depot served as the setting for Dolly's return to Yonkers in the film *Hello, Dolly!*

Garrison is one stop for a mostly country-road walk to Boscobel, the Federal-style restoration located between here and Cold Spring, this next stop providing a shorter but busier road walk to the Hudson River mansion. Cold Spring, an eighteenth- and nineteenth-century river town, is a most attractive destination in itself for restaurants, bed-and-breakfast inns, the Hudson House, antiques and collectibles stores, as well as the boarding station at the end of the Hudson Highlands hike (see Escape 14).

North of Cold Spring, the train dives into a short tunnel beneath Breakneck Ridge. At the Breakneck station, another hikers' stop for two morning weekend trains (see Escape 14), look left for the ruins of Bannerman's, a mock nineteenth-century castle set on Pollepel Island. It was built by a New York arms merchant, and operated as a country retreat and arsenal until an explosion destroyed the place, creating the stabilized New York State ruin you see today.

Beacon is a stop for the hike up Mount Beacon (see Escape 15) and the end of another hike that begins at Breakneck Ridge. I–84 crosses the Hudson here to Newburgh on the opposite shore. The train makes one more stop at the hamlet of New Hamburg before the end of Metro-North service at Poughkeepsie. The imposing former New York Central station has visitor information for nearby sites such as Franklin Roosevelt's Hyde Park house, wife Eleanor's cottage across the road, and the Culinary Institute of America, one of the leading U.S. cooking schools. The CIA also operates several excellent restaurants that are open to the public. Reservations are highly recommended.

For More Information

Metro-North Railroad: (212) 532–4900 (from New York City); (800) 638–7646 (outside the city); www.mta.info.

See Appendix B for information on how to contact any of the establishments listed here.

Resources

Transportation

New York City Transit Authority
(718) 330–1234
www.mta.info
MTA Staten Island Railway
(718) 966–7478
Pay a flat single fare regardless of distance for all subways, local buses, and the Staten Island Railway. There are free transfers (within two hours) between subway and bus and intersecting bus lines. You cannot leave the subway system and enter again without paying an additional fare.

You can also buy MetroCards. Choose from a pay-per-ride card or a one-, seven-, or thirty-day unlimited ride version. For MetroCard information, call (212) 638–7622 or (212) METRO–CARD (in New York City); outside the city, call (800) 638–7622 or (800) METRO–CARD.

Roosevelt Island Tramway
www.ny.com/transportation/
ri_tramway.html
Flat token fare.

Metro-North Railroad
(212) 532–4900 (in New York City)
(800) METRO–INFO
www.mta.info
Hudson Line trains leave from Grand Central Terminal at Park Avenue and 42nd Street, between Lexington and Vanderbilt Avenues. It's open: 5:05 A.M. to 1:30 A.M. Fares vary according to distance. Peak times are considered to be between 5:00 and 10:00 A.M. for trains arriving at Grand Central, and from 4:00 to 8:00 P.M. for departures. Otherwise, off-peak rates apply. Round-trip fares are double one-way. Senior citizens (65 and older) can take 50 percent off one-way peak fares, except for trains arriving between 5:00 and 10:00 A.M. There's an on-board service charge of $2.00 if ticket offices are open.

Circle Line Sightseeing Cruises
Pier 83
West 42nd Street and Twelfth Avenue
New York, NY 10036
(212) 563–3200
www.circleline.com
This is the only cruise line that circles Manhattan Island, with a three-hour narrated Full Island Cruise, a two-hour Semi-Circle Cruise, a two-hour evening Harbor Lights Cruise, various seasonal live music cruises, and the BEAST, a thirty-minute thrill ride.

Staten Island Ferry
(718) 815–2628
www.nyc.gov/calldot
www.siferry.com
Free—no fare for pedestrians or bicycles.

NY Waterway ferries
(800) 53–FERRY
www.nywaterway.com
The flat fare varies according to the route; some ferry fares include connecting NY Waterway bus routes.

PATH
(800) 234–7284
www.pathrail.com
www.panynj.gov
Flat fare, cash machines, and turnstiles.

New Jersey Transit
(973) 762–5100 (outside New Jersey)
(800) 772–2222 (in New Jersey)
www.njtransit.com
Fares vary according to distance. One-way fare is valid at all times; there are round-trip excursion fares during off-peak hours.

Hudson-Bergen Line Rail
(973) 762–5100
(800) 626–7433
www.njtransit.com
Now operates between two terminals in Bayonne north through Liberty State Park to Exchange Place and Newport (Pavonia), Jersey City, and to Hoboken.

Port Authority bus information
(212) 564–8484
This is the general number for all bus services.

Coach USA, Short Line Bus, International Bus Services
(800) 631–8405
www.shortlinebus.com/
From Port Authority to Bear Mountain (Route 2525) offers a travel time of an hour and a half. There are two morning buses up (two and a half hours apart), and two afternoon buses back (two hours apart).

Red and Tan Bus Lines
(212) 279–6526
www.redandtanlines.com
Route 9A–9W runs from the Port Authority Bus Terminal to Alpine, Closter Dock Road, Route 9W (forty minutes); and from George Washington Bridge Bus Station to Alpine, Closter Dock Road, and Route 9W (twenty minutes).

Suburban Transit Co.
(800) 222–0492
www.suburbantransit.com
Hourly bus on Sunday, more frequent on Saturday, from Kingston, New Jersey, to Port Authority (one hour, forty minutes) or to Princeton–Palmer Square (ten minutes).

Westchester County Bee-Line Bus
(914) 813–7777
www.beelinebus.com/

Bicycle Policies on Local Transportation
New York City Subway: Bikes permitted at all times. No permit required. Out of courtesy, avoid rush hours.

Roosevelt Island Tramway: Bicycles permitted at all times. No permit required.

Metro-North (212–532–4900): $5.00 permits at window 27, Grand Central Terminal. Bicycles are okay all week, but not during rush hours. The limit is two bikes per car; a maximum of four per train. On weekends, special bike trains are marked with a bicycle symbol. Two morning departures northbound and two afternoon southbound (also stopping at Manitou and Breakneck) will take a maximum of fifteen bikes per train.

Long Island Rail Road
(718–558–8228): $5.00 permits available at Penn Station or Grand Central Terminal. Same access at Metro-North, but some summer weekend restrictions.

New Jersey Transit (973–762–5100): No permit needed for trains; no bikes on buses. No bikes during morning rush hours to New York or afternoon rush hours to New Jersey. No bikes on some holidays. Bungee cord required.

PATH (800–234–PATH or 201–216–6247): No permit needed. No restrictions on weekends and holidays. No bicycles during inbound and outbound rush hours.

Sunrise Coach Lines (North Fork Long Island/Shelter Island; 516–477–1200): $10 for carriage in the luggage bay.

Hampton Jitney (South Fork/ Hamptons/Sag Harbor; 800–936–0440): $10 for carriage in the luggage bay.

Staten Island Ferry (718–815–BOAT): No charge; enter on lower level.

New York Waterways (800–533–3779): $1.00 fee. Bike okay at all times. Limit two per boat on most runs.

Bicycles on Bridges/Ferries

East River: Brooklyn, Manhattan, Williamsburg, Queensboro, Triboro.

Harlem River: Wards Island Pedestrian Bridge (open daylight hours April through October), Triboro, Willis Avenue, Third Avenue, Madison Avenue, 145th Street, Macombs Dam, Washington, University Heights, Broadway.

Hudson River: George Washington Bridge only within New York City, otherwise NY Waterway ferry; Bear Mountain Bridge.

New York Harbor Crossing: Staten Island Ferry from Lower Manhattan to St. George, Staten Island. *No* bikes on Verrazano-Narrows Bridge.

Regional Organizations, Resources, and Destinations

Citywide Organizations

Big Apple Greeter
1 Centre Street, Suite 2035
New York, NY 10007
(212) 669–8159
Fax: (212) 669–3685
www.bigapplegreeter.org
A free service that connects friendly New York City volunteers with visitors for visits of neighborhoods by foot, subway, and bus. Shows the visitor, individuals, or families a neighborhood through the eyes of a New Yorker. Advance notice is required.

Gateway National Recreation Area
Floyd Bennett Field
Brooklyn, NY 11231
(718) 338–3799

**Historic House Trust of
New York City**
The Arsenal Room 203, Central Park,
830 Fifth Avenue
New York, NY 10021
(212) 360–8282
Fax: (212) 360–8201
www.preserve.org/hht
Preserves and promotes historic house
museums located in New York City parks
in all five boroughs, in a public-private
partnership with the city of New York
Parks and Recreation. Call or write for a
free brochure.

Manhattan: Dyckman Farmhouse
Museum (212–304–9422); www.dyck
man.org.

Little Red Lighthouse: Inwood Urban
Park Rangers (212–304–2365).

Brooklyn: Lefferts Homestead
(718–789–2822).

Staten Island: Alice Austen House
Museum (718–816–4506);
www.aliceausten.8m.com

**NYC & Company
New York Convention & Visitors
Bureau**
810 Seventh Avenue (at 53rd Street)
New York, NY 10019
(212) 484–1200
www.nycvisit.com

Times Square Visitors Center
1560 Broadway
(between 46th and 47th Streets)
(212) 768–1560
www.timesquarebid.org
Open daily 8:00 A.M. to 8:00 P.M.

Grand Central Terminal
42nd Street and Park Avenue
www.grandcentralterminal.com
Main Concourse, first window in eastern
bank of ticket windows, near ramp up to
Vanderbilt Hall. Open Monday through
Saturday, 9:00 A.M. to 9:00 P.M.; Sunday,
9:30 A.M. to 6:00 P.M.

Pennsylvania Station
32nd Street and Seventh Avenue
Amtrak Passenger service level.
Visitors' Center open 9:00 A.M. to 4:30 P.M.

Transportation Alternatives
115 West 30th Street, Suite 1207
New York, NY 10001
(212) 629–8080
www.transalt.org
New York City advocacy group for cyclists,
pedestrians, and transit users. A
$30.00 membership brings a quarterly
magazine, *Transportation Alternatives*, with
news, information, discounts at bike
stores, and invitations to T.A. events.
Cycling route maps available for all five
boroughs show off-street paths, on-street
bike lanes, recommended on-street routes,
and detailed access to bridge crossings.

Bookstores/Publications
Hagstrom Map and Travel Center
57 West 43rd Street
New York, NY 10036
(212) 398–1222
Hagstrom maps for the Tristate region by
borough and by county, New York–New
Jersey Trail Conference maps, and local
guide books.

Rand McNally Map & Travel Store

150 East 52nd Street
New York, NY 10022
(212) 758–7488
A comprehensive selection of maps, guidebooks, and travel accoutrements for destinations worldwide.

New York Magazine

www.newyorkmetro.com
A weekly with what's going on.

New York Times

Friday weekend section, Sunday City section, Arts.

Time Out New York

www.timeoutny.com
New York City arts and entertainment listings.

Manhattan

Alliance for Downtown New York

120 Broadway, Suite 3340
New York, NY 10271
(212) 566–6700
www.downtownny.com
Check the Web site for updates on the status of downtown Manhattan. Other information includes tourist attractions, a comprehensive calendar of events, directories of restaurants, shops, and services, and transportation options.

Battery Park City Authority

1 World Financial Center
New York, NY 10281
(212) 417–2000
www.batteryparkcity.org
Ninety-two acres of residential, commercial, and open spaces. Restaurants, museum, schools, events, shopping on the Hudson River.

Chelsea Piers Sports & Entertainment Complex

23rd Street and the Hudson
New York, NY 10011
(212) 336–6800
www.chelseapiers.com
A thirty-acre sports village featuring a golf driving range, roller and ice rinks, an aggressive skate park, a bowling center, batting cages, and facilities for gymnastics, rock climbing, soccer, and basketball. On-site restaurants, dining cruises, and sports shops.

The Cloisters—The Metropolitan Museum

Fort Tryon Park
New York, NY 10040
(212) 923–3700
www.metmuseum.org
A Metropolitan Museum branch exhibiting medieval art and architecture.

Dyckman Farmhouse Museum

(212) 304–9422
Historic House Trust of New York City:
(212) 360–8282
www.nyc.gov/parks or
www.preserve.org/hht

Hudson River Park Trust

Pier 40 (foot of West Houston Street and West Street)
(917) 661–8740
www.HudsonRiverPark.org

Intrepid Sea-Air-Space Museum

West 46th Street and Hudson River
(212) 245–0072
www.intrepidmuseum.com

Metropolitan Waterfront Alliance
457 Madison Avenue
New York, NY 10022
(800) 364–9943
www.waterwire.net

**Museum of Jewish Heritage—A
Living Memorial to the Holocaust**
18 First Place, Battery Park City
New York, NY 10004
(212) 509–6130
www.mjhnyc.org
The twentieth-century Jewish experience
before, during, and after the Holocaust as
described through personal accounts, arti-
facts, photos, and film.

Passenger Ship Terminal
West 48th through 52nd Streets and
Hudson River
For ship arrivals and departures, visit
www.nypst.com; the World Ship Society
site for port news, arrivals, and departures
is at www.worldshipny.com.

Riverbank State Park
West 137th through West 145th Streets
and Hudson River
(212) 694–3600
Twenty-eight acres, 69 feet above the
Hudson River. You'll find an Olympic-
sized swimming pool, covered skating rink
(ice and roller), four tennis courts, four
hand/paddle tennis courts, four basketball
courts, a softball field, and a 400-meter
running track around a football and soccer
field.

**Roosevelt Island Information
Roosevelt Island Operating
Corporation:** www.rioc.com

Roosevelt Island News Wire:
www.nyc10044.com

Roosevelt Island Tramway:
www.rioc.com/transportation.html

Skyscraper Museum
South end of Battery Park City
(212) 968–1961
www.skyscraper.org

Bronx

Bronx information
www.bronx.ny.us

The Bronx County Historical Society
3309 Bainbridge Avenue
Bronx, NY 10467
(718) 881–8900
www.bronxhistoricalsociety.org
History of the Bronx and New York City:
book publisher, exhibits, tours, educa-
tional programs, conferences, lectures.

New York Botanical Garden
200th Street and Kazimiroff Boulevard
(Bronx River Parkway at Fordham Road)
Bronx, NY 10458–5126
(718) 817–8700
www.nybg.org
One of America's foremost public gardens
and a National Historic Landmark. Look
for the *World of Plants* exhibit (from the
rain forests to the deserts) in the newly
reopened Enid A. Haupt Conservatory.

Wildlife Conservation Society (formerly New York Zoological Society)
2300 Southern Boulevard
Bronx, NY 10460
(718) 220–5100
www.wcs.org

Queens

Chamber of Commerce of the Rockaways, Inc.
253 Beach 116th Street
Rockaway Park, NY 11694
(718) 634–1300
Fax: (718) 634–9623
www.rockawaychamberofcommerce.com
A partnership of professionals, civic associations, and residents working together to maintain and improve business, quality of life, tourism, recreation, and the arts in the Rockaways' unique "beach to bay" environment.

Jamaica Bay Wildlife Refuge
(718) 318–4340
www.brooklynbirdclub.org/jamaica.htm or
www.fieldtrip.com/ny/83184340.htm

Brooklyn

Astroland
Coney Island
(718) 265–2100
www.astroland.com

Brighton Beach
Brighton Neighborhood Association
1121 Brighton Beach Avenue
Brooklyn, NY 11235
(718) 891–0800
www.brightonbeach.com or
www.brightonbeachbid.com
Source of tourism information for the area.

Brooklyn Botanic Garden
1000 Washington Avenue
Brooklyn, NY 11225
(718) 623–7200
www.bbg.org

Fifty-two acres of display gardens, an indoor conservatory, and events for all ages.

Brooklyn Bridge
www.nyctourist.com/bridge1.htm
www.nycroads.crossings/brooklyn

Brooklyn Cyclones
Coney Island
(718) 449–8497
www.brooklyncyclones.com
The Brooklyn Cyclones are a New York Mets farm team in the New York–Penn League (short-season Class A); the Staten Island Yankees are in the same league. KeySpan Park is located between the surf and the boardwalk, between West 17th and West 18th.

BRIC/Brooklyn Information & Culture
647 Fulton Street
Brooklyn, NY 11217
(718) 855–7882
www.brooklynx.org
Information on Brooklyn's museums, parks, arts, cultural institutions, and sites of special interest by mail and on the Web site. Free quarterly calendar. Closed weekends. Oversees the Brooklyn Tourism Council.

Brooklyn information
www.brooklynonline.com

Brooklyn Museum of Art
200 Eastern Parkway
Brooklyn, NY 11238
(718) 638–5000
www.brooklynart.org
The second largest museum in New York

City, featuring art from ancient Egypt to contemporary. Gift shop, bookstore, food service.

Coney Island
www.coneyisland.org

Gateway National Recreation Area
Floyd Bennett Field
Brooklyn, NY 11231
(718) 338–3799

Jamaica Bay Wildlife Refuge
(718) 318–4340
www.brooklynbirdclub.org/jamaica.htm or www.fieldtrip.com/ny/83184340.htm

Lefferts Homestead
Prospect Park
(718) 789–2822

New York Aquarium
West 8th Street at Surf Avenue
Brooklyn, NY 11224
(718) 265–FISH or (718) 265–3400
www.nyaquarium.com
Three hundred species, fourteen acres, daily dolphin shows, up-close walrus encounters. Gift shop, restaurant, parking.

Prospect Park
(718) 965–8999
www.prospectpark.org

Prospect Park Wildlife Center
(718) 399–7339

***Dorothy B VIII* Sheepshead Bay**
Pier 6, Emmons Avenue
(718) 646–4057
www.dorothyb.com
This fishing boat sails at 7:00 A.M. Adults $35, seniors $32, children $20; bait and

rod included, tackle extra. Blackfish, cod, ling, mackerel, sea bass.

Gage & Tollner, Inc.
372 Fulton Street
Brooklyn, NY 11201
(718) 875–5181
www.gageandtollner.com
Steaks, chops, and seafood. Opened in 1879, this is the oldest landmark restaurant in New York. Victorian decor, working gas lamps.

Junior's Restaurant
386 Flatbush Avenue Extension at DeKalb Avenue
Brooklyn, NY 11201
(718) 852–5257
www.juniorscheesecake.com
Dining room, counter, takeout. New York specialties.

Lundy Bros. Restaurant
1901 Emmons Avenue
Sheepshead Bay
(718) 743–0022
www.lundybros.com
Seafood.

Peter Luger Steak House
178 Broadway
Brooklyn, NY 11211
(718) 387–7400
www.peterluger.com
Cash only, no credit cards. Steaks!

Staten Island

Alice Austen House Museum
2 Hylan Boulevard
Staten Island, NY 10305
(718) 816–4506
www.aliceausten.8m.com

nyc.gov/html/si/html/4.html
Historic house museum at the entrance to
New York Harbor on Staten Island. Tours
of the 1690 landmark home, gift shop.
Open noon to 5:00 P.M. Closed Monday
through Wednesday, and January and
February.

**Council on the Arts and Humanities
for Staten Island**
(718) 447–3329
www.statenislandarts.org

Fort Wadsworth
(718) 354–4500

National Lighthouse Museum
(718) 556–1681
www.lighthousemuseum.org

Staten Island Ferry Information
(718) 815–BOAT
www.siferry.com/

Staten Island Railway Information
(718) 966–7478
www.mta.nyc.ny.us/nyct/sir

Staten Island Tourist Information
www.statenislandusa.com/

Staten Island Yankees
Richmond County Bank Ballpark
(718) 720–9265
www.siyanks.com

Hudson River Valley
Bear Mountain State Park and Inn
State park: (845) 786–2701
www.hudsonriver.com/bearmtn.htm
Bear Mountain Inn: (845) 786–2731

www.bearmountaininn.com
Open 365 days. There's skating from late
October to mid-March; the pool is open
from Memorial Day through Labor Day.
Hessian Lake offers paddleboats and rowboats for hire. There's also a zoo and interpretive center. Parking costs $5.00.

Culinary Institute of America
Hyde Park, NY
(845) 471–6608
www.ciachef.edu

Hudson House (Inn)
2 Main Street
Cold Spring, NY 10516
(845) 265–9355
www.hudsonhouseinn.com

Pig Hill Inn
73 Main Street
Cold Spring, NY 10516
(845) 265–9247
www.pighillinn.com

Boscobel Restoration
Garrison, NY
(845) 265–3638
www.boscobel.org

Historic Hudson River
www.hhr.highlands.com
History, culture, and conservation of the
Hudson River Valley.

Historic Hudson Valley
150 White Plains Road
Tarrytown, NY 10591
(914) 631–8200
www.hudsonvalley.org
Historic Hudson Valley's properties
include Kykuit (the Rockefeller estate);

Lyndhurst (between Irvington and Tarrytown); Montgomery Place; Philipsburg Manor (Sleepy Hollow); Sunnyside (Irvington); Union Church of Pocantico Hills (Tarrytown); and Van Cortlandt Manor (Croton-on-Hudson). The Web site also has links to Philipse Manor (Yonkers) and the Hudson River Museum (Glenwood, Yonkers).

Hudson River
www.hudsonriver.com
Here's the site to visit for information on the historic river towns of Westchester: from south to north, Yonkers, Hastings-on-Hudson, Dobbs Ferry, Irvington, Tarrytown, Sleepy Hollow, Ossining, Croton-on-Hudson, and Cortlandt.

Hyde Park Chamber of Commerce
www.hydeparkchamber.org/
Information on the Franklin Delano Roosevelt home, Val-Kill Cottage (Eleanor Roosevelt's home), Mills Mansion, Vanderbilt Mansion, and the Culinary Institute of America, with links to Dutchess County Tourism.

New York State Parks, Recreation and Historic Preservation
www.nysparks.state.ny.us/

Old Croton (Aqueduct) Trailway State Park
15 Walnut Street
Dobbs Ferry, NY 10522
(914) 693–5259
www.hudsonriver.com
Friends of the Old Croton Aqueduct sell detailed full-color maps for $5.50. Visit the Web site or write to the above address.

West Point Military Academy
(914) 938–2638
www.usma.edu
Tours.

New York–New Jersey (Bistate)

Appalachian Mountain Club
5 Tudor City Place
New York, NY 10017
(212) 986–1430
Fax: (212) 986–1432
New York–New Jersey Web site: amc-ny.org

New York–New Jersey Trail Conference
156 Ramapo Valley Road (Route 202)
Mahwah, NJ 07430
(201) 512–9348
www.nynjtc.org/

Palisades Interstate Park Commission
Bear Mountain State Park
Bear Mountain, NY 10911–0427
(845) 786–2701
www.pipc.org/

PIPC, New Jersey Section
P.O. Box 155
Alpine, NJ 07620
(201) 768–1360
Long Path map and excellent description.

New Jersey

Delaware & Raritan Canal State Park
625 Canal Road
Somerset, NJ 08873
(732) 873–3050
www.dandrcanal.com

Hoboken

www.hoboken.com or www.hobokeni.com

Arthur's Tavern

237 Washington Street (at 3rd)
Hoboken, NJ
(201) 656–5009

Helmers'

1036 Washington Street (at 11th)
Hoboken, NJ
(201) 963–3333

Spring Lake Chamber of Commerce

P.O. Box 694
Spring Lake, NJ 07762
(732) 449–0577
www.springlake.org

Ashling Cottage

106 Sussex Avenue
Spring Lake, NJ 07762
(732) 449–3553 or (888) 274–5464
www.Ashlingcottage.com

Normandy Inn

21 Tuttle Avenue
Spring Lake, NJ 07762
(732) 449–7172 or (800) 449–1888
www.normandyinn.com

Sandpiper Inn

7 Atlantic Avenue
Spring Lake, NJ 07762
(732) 449–6060 or (800) 824–2779
Dining.

Spring Lake Pizzeria

1110 Third Avenue
(732) 449–9595
Italian menu.

Ocean Grove Chamber of Commerce

P.O. Box 415
Ocean Grove, NJ 07756
(732) 774–1391
www.oceangrovenj.com/

Ocean Grove Camp Meeting Association

www.oceangrove.org/
Links to several related sites: www.
oceangrove.org/links.htm

Carol Inn B&B

11 Pitman Avenue
Ocean Grove, NJ 07756
(732) 502–0303
Fax: (732) 776–6174

Ocean Plaza Hotel

18 Ocean Pathway
Ocean Grove, NJ 07756
(732) 774–6552 or (888) 891–9442
www.ogplaza.com/seeyou.htm

Captain Jack's

68 Main Street
Ocean Grove, NJ 07756
(732) 869–0770
Run by the owners of Ocean Plaza.

Nagles Apothecary Café

43 Main Street
Ocean Grove, NJ 07756
(732) 776–9797

About the Author

Ted Scull has been hiking and cycling about New York and outlying districts since moving to Manhattan in the mid-1960s. He first worked for a shipping line, then shifted to education where he was a teacher, guidance counselor, and principal in independent schools. For several years, he commuted to work by bicycle through Central Park. Since 1980, he has been a full-time travel writer and an author of eight books published on ocean liner travel, worldwide cruising, day and weekend trips from New York, local excursions by water, and specialized New York City topics.

Over the years, he has led several hundred hikes throughout the five boroughs and into the nearby tristate region. In almost every case, the trips were made by subway, bus, train, or ferry, encouraging the participants to seek out other destinations using the region's excellent public transportation network.

Worldwide travels include all fifty states, about half of South America, most of Europe, and large parts of Asia, Africa, Australasia, and the Antarctic Peninsula. He has lived in Paris and London and worked at a medical mission in Tanganyika. He looks for great hikes wherever he travels—from the Southwest Coastal Path in England to a walking safari in South Africa and a national park in Queensland.

Ted holds an M.A. in history from the University of London, an M.S. in education from Bank Street College, New York, and a B.A. in history from Trinity College, Hartford. He is married to Suellyn, an Australian who works in education administration. They currently and forever expect to live in Manhattan.